Toward College Success:

Is Your Teenager Ready, Willing, and Able?

P. Carol Jones and Patricia Wilkins-Wells

Langdon Street Press

Langdon Street Press
212 3rd Avenue North, Suite 290
Minneapolis, MN 55401
612.455.2293
www.langdonstreetpress.com

ISBN-13: 978-1-936782-08-6
LCCN: 2011925321

Distributed by Itasca Books

Cover Design and Typeset by Kyle Wyatt

Printed in the United States of America

Toward College Success:

Is Your Teenager Ready, Willing, and Able?

Contents

Acknowledgments

This book was in the making during the many years that my cowriter, the late Patricia Wilkins-Wells, fretted over her students at the University of Northern Colorado who seemed to have started college with little idea of how to succeed. It was Pat's desire to push parents to prepare their students for a successful college experience that inspired this book; so first, I thank Pat for her insight and dedication, and for letting me join her in the effort.

Thanks to the numerous students, parents, teachers, administrators, and law enforcement personnel who shared their stories. Your experiences are what make this book work.

Many thanks to the people who read and commented on the book: Kate Thomsen, Joyce Caufman, Krista Caufman, Darlene Mueller Morse, Pat Parker, and Beth Eikenbary. Your comments improved every page.

A big thanks to Betty Stewart for her edit—you greatly improved the book!

I give a special thanks to Pat's beloved daughter, Katie, and her husband, John, who encouraged me to finish the book after Pat's death. Your support gave me what I needed to continue.

And I must thank my own students—Luke, Wes, and Mallory—for providing me with (too many?) stories for this book. Despite your father's and my fumbling parenting efforts, I really think all three of you are "ready, willing, and able" for whatever comes your way.

In memory of Pat Wilkins-Wells.

Introduction

It's the week before finals and you've been asking your sixteen-year-old every day if he has started studying. His response: "They haven't told us anything yet." What "they" have told him is that he has two major tests on Thursday and a chemistry lab due on Friday. In addition, he has dress rehearsal for the opening of a community production that will run every night through his finals. He comes home at 11 p.m. from rehearsal, completely exhausted and with at least two hours of homework before him. He cries to you that it is all too much and that he'll probably lose his B in math after he flunks the test the next day. You try to talk to him about time management and priorities, but he notoriously waits until the last minute on all his schoolwork. He is a sophomore—two and a half years before college. Will he be ready with effective time management skills?

It's parent-teacher conferences and you listen to your ninth-grade daughter's English teacher's report of four missed assignments and Cs and Ds on all her tests. The teacher also informs you that your daughter is behind on a major writing assignment that is due on Monday. When you confront your daughter she swears she turned in some of those assignments, the others she missed because she was absent, and the reason she does so poorly on tests is that her teacher doesn't like her. She is four years away from college. Will she be willing to take responsibility in time?

Your daughter is registering for her senior year and she is having a hard time fitting her beloved choir classes, for which she has yet to audition, into a schedule that must include government, English, math, science, and history—all required for graduation. After two meetings with her counselor, her advisor verbally agrees to hold open the choir slots while your daughter auditions. Your daughter, excited with selection into her preferred choir, never returns to the counselor's office after the auditions.

Weeks later, you get a call from the school asking if your daughter has dropped out because she never registered. She did not follow through after choir selection and her counselor was busy with other schedules. Consequently she couldn't get into a government class and has to take it in the summer to fulfill graduation requirements. She's off to college after the next summer. Will she be able to ask questions, follow through, and be her own advocate?

It is difficult enough maneuvering through your child's teenage years without wondering if he or she will be ready, willing, and able to succeed in college, but wonder you should. If college is the goal of your student, that student needs to be mature enough, resilient enough, and confident enough to face life in a dorm room, conflicts with roommates, bureaucracy deadlines, and a more demanding academic setting. That student probably will be giddy with more freedoms and overwhelmed with more responsibilities than ever before at the very time he or she is supposed to cull a college education, a degree, and the beginnings of a successful career. Much as parents hate to admit it, the truth is that in spite of their best efforts and intentions, failure is possible, even for the best and brightest of high school graduates. For anyone raising children, the implications of this fact can be staggering. Most parents fervently believe that their children's entire future may be at stake, and at no small financial or emotional cost to everyone involved. So how do parents make the decisions necessary to assure a successful outcome?

Parents obviously cannot control many of the things they would like to control when it comes to their children. Parents do not even control some of the things in their children's lives—such as where they go and don't go, and with whom—that they sometimes think they do. However, looking at the experiences of today's families it is clear that some students arrive at college better prepared than others—and they're prepared for more than just academics. The real question parents need to be asking, long before the end of high school, is whether their children are, or will be, ready, willing, and able to attend college within a few months after they receive their diploma, and, if not, what does that mean? This book is an attempt to help answer those questions.

Many parents of adolescents know that a cooperative, enthusiastic, sharing sixth grader can turn into a confrontational, apathetic, secretive teenager overnight; then come to Mom or Dad overwhelmed with some issue the next day wanting love, understanding, and reassurance. Those turbulent emotions can directly affect a student's experiences at school. We all hope that things will work out, but life holds no guarantees and no one wants to put forward literally thousands of dollars for their child's college education only to discover that the student was not prepared—something we parents might have figured out earlier and in time to remedy.

The problem, however, is that being a parent does not in itself give us the ability to know in advance all that our young adults will encounter. This is not to say there is a lack of relevant reading materials for college-bound high schoolers and their parents. Far from it. A visit to the local bookstore or library will present you with a number of books addressing such topics as college admissions requirements, financing your student's education, how to survive the college years, and the necessary emotional adjustments you and your child should anticipate. However, many of the challenges involved in successfully adjusting to college life need to be addressed much earlier than the college orientation program for incoming freshmen in the summer before they begin classes. Taking responsibility, managing time, self-advocating, and setting realistic goals are skills that eighteen-year-olds cannot learn overnight. This book, therefore, is to add to these existing resources an overview of the issues concerned in actually preparing students for college while they are in high school or earlier. If parents can actively prepare their kids for this transition during these earlier years, there is a much greater likelihood that once the financial and academic issues have been dealt with, they will actually succeed.

This idea of preparing the student for the college environment, rather than the other way around, irritates or even angers some parents. They argue that it is the responsibility of the colleges and universities to create an environment that is "user friendly." When parents pay school tuition and fees, they point out that they have become consumers who should have the right to demand the services for which they have paid. Fair enough, and it is important to note that because education at this level operates in a competitive market, many, if not all, schools make a real effort to use updated studies on student life in reforming existing school policies and practices or in creating new ones with the goal of boosting student success rates. However, changes in school policies and programs can take years to formulate and even more years to actually take effect. Colleges and universities are, after all, complex institutions, and meaningful changes take years to materialize. But parents need to understand that even the most user-friendly colleges cannot be expected to spoon-feed or coddle students to ensure the school's popularity as an institution or to ensure their students' success. Some would argue that this is actually doing a disservice to students since such coddling does not realistically prepare students for the world of work. Colleges and universities that maintain high standards and academic rigor serve students well. Relaxed rules and understanding professors may feel better, but in the long run, students' learning and preparation for life may suffer.

In the meantime, our kids continue year by year to approach college age, and it seems only realistic that parents need to know how to prepare their teenaged students now, regardless of what those future policy changes may bring. Instead of parents' hoping for the perfect college environment for their kids, this book takes the position that parents should take responsibility to prepare their students for the less-than-perfect college, and world, that those students will inhabit in the not-so-distant future.

Since most of us tend to look to our own experiences and those of the people around us rather than reading academic journal articles, it seemed most logical to listen to people's experiences directly through a series of interviews and to report those experiences. Over the next nine chapters, this book will show you the ways in which families and their students have struggled with a range of issues and challenges, some of which represent success stories and others not. Those issues and challenges will include some familiar ones such as grades, sex, and alcohol, but also some less obvious or less well-known ones such as new privacy laws or the fact that the vast majority of today's students are working at various jobs while going to school. You also will hear from some of the people who work directly with those students and families: from dorm supervisors and their assisting staff, to law enforcement personnel, to mental health counselors, and others. Whenever possible, detailed personal stories are included (names or revealing specifics changed or omitted) in the hope that by doing so readers will be able to find the situations and personalities to which they can best relate. Since denial seems to be a problem for many of us—"What, my child?"—such stories may help in overcoming that problem as well. Each chapter ends with a section titled "Preparing Your Teenager," where you will find example scenarios detailing how to approach common challenges.

Chapter 1

College Success Requires Maturity:
Is Your Teenager Ready, and Are You?

Most parents send their students off to college assuming—or with fingers crossed—that they have matured enough through their high school years to handle conflicts, to make safe decisions, and to generally take care of themselves. After all, at age eighteen they are legally adults, and their parents have done their best to teach them the basics: right from wrong, good manners, being responsible. In short, these children have been shaped into well-adjusted, mature young adults. Or have they? Despite parents' best intentions, sometimes their teenager has not developed the maturity he or she needs to handle conflicts with a roommate, to take seriously the investment made, or to know when she or he is overwhelmed. Regardless of why that may be, it is important to be realistic about your teenager's maturity and readiness for college before she fills out college applications. Remember, she will be on her own for probably the first time in her life and facing situations she has never faced before. Is she ready?

How responsible are eighteen-year-olds?

Back in the 1960s and early 1970s, when baby boomers went to college, the old concept of *in loco parentis* was still a lingering reality on some college campuses. The idea was that colleges were, at least in part, supposed to operate as substitute parents for students while they were enrolled. This was the argument behind "closing hours" for dorms (mostly women's dorms), separate housing for men and women, bed checks in the middle of the night, and the often dreaded envelopes at the end of

1

freshman semesters informing parents of students' grades. In spite of the fact that, back then, there were proportionately fewer young people who went on to college after high school than there are today, the fact that an eighteen-year-old was still in school meant he or she was in some ways still a child.

Beginning in the mid- to late 1960s, however, things shifted. Not only have school policies changed, but so has the law. Housing is often coed, or partially so, with both sexes sharing a building, sharing the same wing of a building, or, in some cases, occupying rooms commingled on the same floor. Although policies vary from school to school, many colleges and universities allow students to have overnight visitors of the opposite sex in their rooms, requiring only that they sign in at the desk. Hardly any dorms today have the traditionally hated closing hours. The most significant changes, perhaps, are the two areas in which recent privacy laws have severely limited the discretion a school may use to inform parents about their student's situation: the legislation known as FERPA (Family Education and Right to Privacy Act) and HIPAA (Health, Information, Portability, and Accountability Act). As·we discuss more fully in Chapter 7, under these privacy laws, unless your student signs specific release forms both for the school and for medical services (the local hospital and campus health center), your call to inquire about your student's welfare may well follow the path in the following story.

Jean and Bob had not heard from their daughter, Emily, for more than three weeks. Repeated efforts to call her on both her dorm room phone and her cell phone had failed. Frantic late-night messages went unanswered. Jean and Bob knew Emily's roommate's name was Heather, an English major from Houston, but they knew little more than that. Emily had been dating a junior engineering student who lived off-campus, but efforts to contact him using a telephone number listed in the campus directory produced only a "no longer in service" message. Feeling a little embarrassed, but also exasperated, Bob called the hall supervisor of the dorm.

The hall supervisor told Bob that all she could do was conduct a "welfare check"—meaning that the supervisor would look into the situation and then encourage Emily to call her parents. No, the supervisor could not tell them if Emily had been sleeping elsewhere. No, she could not tell them if Emily had been going to class. No, she could not tell them if Emily was seeing a mental health counselor (Emily had experienced some episodes of depression while in high school). Irate, Bob demanded to know why in hell not? To which the supervisor replied, "I am not allowed, by law, to answer your questions, but I really will check and see what I can find out and try to get Emily to call you."

Whether parents are ready for it or not, when their kids turn eighteen years of age, whether they go off to college, work full time in the labor force, or enter the military, they are legal adults and eligible to do most anything except buy alcohol. However, as larger percentages of our nation's young adults are now seeking some kind of post–high school education or training, and are therefore still classified as students, most parents and much of society still tend to think of these young adults as "kids." And with good reason: most still need our financial help, most have never been on their own, and, like the fledglings they are, they still need guidance.

Liam was a freshman at the University of Colorado. His family lived only an hour's drive from campus, but Liam's parents respected his independence and did not pester him to call and come home often. Liam enjoyed his new freedom, but he stayed in semiregular contact with his mom and dad. One morning, nineteen-year-old Liam called his mom with this story: "Mom, I went snowboarding yesterday with some of the guys and landed a jump wrong. I slammed my face into my knees and my nose bled pretty bad. My eye is black-and-blue and real swollen, and my face hurts like hell. Should I go to the health clinic?" Patiently, Mom reminded Liam that they bought the health clinic package just for this sort of thing. "Yes, please, go now," she said. It turned out that Liam had to go to a local hospital for an MRI that showed he had a small facial fracture below his eye.

Despite the fact that Liam and his fellow students still occasionally ask for parental advice, they alone are responsible for themselves. The problem with the image of students as "kids" is that it often contributes to the related idea that somehow college is just an extension of high school. Many parents tend to see colleges as responsible for taking care of their "kids" once the students arrive on campus, or at least see the schools as responsible for keeping track of them and reporting back to parents if there is a problem. Students, as well, tend to see colleges in this light, although they generally assume more personal liberties for themselves than their parents do.

However, and this comes as a surprise to both parents and students more often than one might think, college life is decidedly not the same thing as high school, only larger. Going to a high school party where there are drugs or alcohol present is not the same thing as having a neighbor living four feet away from you who is getting drunk two or three nights a week and/or doing drugs just as often, and insisting on sharing his experiences at 3 or 4 a.m. Having a sexually active friend in high school is not the same thing as having a roommate who repeatedly brings her boyfriend to bed with her in your 12-by-16-foot dorm room during midterm exams. And having a high school friend who sometimes ditches class is not the same thing as knowing that your friend down the hall has not been seen nor heard from in two weeks.

It was obvious from the beginning that Carmen's first-semester freshman-year roommate at Montana State University was a partier. The roommate found a party most nights of the week, drank heavily, then found her way back to the dorm room to sleep it off. Due to her late nights and hangovers, the roommate skipped most of her classes. Although Carmen had been to parties in high school where alcohol was consumed, it was quite a different situation to be living with someone who continually partied and came home drunk four to five nights a week. Carmen was not a drinker and although she tolerated the roommate, it was a very unsatisfactory living condition for her.

College life definitely will present social and emotional changes and challenges for students. Helping them prepare for these changes is essential for their success.

Ready for college or not?

When your student begins college, not only will he have some social, personal lifestyle adjustments to make, but he will have to maneuver through specific academic challenges as well. As incoming freshmen, students will need to be ready, willing, and able to function successfully in an academic bureaucracy. It is up to parents, therefore, to help students get ready for a level of personal responsibility that they are unlikely to have encountered before, or perhaps even imagined. Unfortunately, this is not something parents can accomplish the week before Sarah and Josh head off to school by simply explaining to them the demands they will face, since by this time they often are listening less to Mom and Dad than to anyone and likely would not believe that their parents could offer some useful insight.

Another thing to consider: If your student is already a high school senior and you are fairly certain that he is not ready for such a transition, it may simply mean he needs a bit more time. Going straight to college from high school is not the right road for every student, no matter how much they are pushed in that direction. Objectively evaluate your teenager's readiness and be willing to consider alternative routes to success.

Jackson was a bright, creative student who struggled with ADD. He also experienced bouts of depression and was caught a few times with marijuana in the early years of high school. By the end of his junior year, he had completed all of the courses required for graduation and scored well on several Advanced Placement exams. Jackson's parents felt he had matured since his earlier years of difficulty and was taking more responsibility for himself, although he still found focusing and paying attention to be difficult tasks. When his high school senior year loomed ahead, Jackson's mother grew concerned that the light load of courses he was choosing to take as a senior would not stimulate his active, quick mind. For several weeks, she suggested he finish high school the following December, then take a few months to do volunteer service somewhere in the world. Slowly, Jackson came around to the idea. Things fell into place and Jackson and his college-attending brother are lined up to volunteer for three months with a conservation organization in Peru. In the meantime, Jackson filled out a couple of college applications. Not surprisingly, Jackson recently told his mother he just isn't sure about going to college.

"Everything that is hard for me in school—sitting for a long time in a classroom and listening to someone lecture—is what worries me about college," Jackson told his mom. "I don't know what I want to do, but I don't want more of boring classroom time."

Now Jackson and his mom are exploring the idea of him postponing his college career. Once he returns from Peru, hopefully with new insights and ideas, he is considering taking a few classes at a local community college while he decides if college is right for him and, if so, when to go.

Keep in mind that it is never too late for your student to go to school, as long as you are willing to admit that she may be one of the many thousands of students who take a somewhat unconventional path through academia.

Not only are there a myriad of different college environments available to suit your student's personal needs, but the numbers of "nontraditional students"—those who spend a few years working, growing, and learning before returning to campuses to complete their degrees—continues to expand as well.

Gabe was a bright student who made high marks in high school, until his senior year. His mother, Alice, said he had taken all his required courses and was basically coasting his final year, bored with school and its lack of academic challenges. Making things worse, Gabe started experimenting with alcohol and marijuana and hanging with a crowd of kids who felt they were wasting their time in high school. With less than three months to graduate, Gabe, at age eighteen, dropped out of school.

Gabe did decide to test for a general education diploma (GED). "He just went and took the test without any preparation," Alice said. "He scored so high that he received a letter praising his good efforts."

But it wasn't until Gabe was twenty-one that Alice and her husband were able to convince him to try college. Gabe entered a two-year community college and "loved it," Alice said. Gabe eagerly and successfully went on to study and complete a degree in microbiology at a four-year university.

While you ponder your student's readiness to attend college, take an honest look at your child and home environment, and determine his strengths and needs, but also what may hinder his success in college. Academic advisors, mental health counselors, faculty members, and campus police whom we interviewed all pointed to two basic home situations that can lead directly to academic failure: situations of privilege and neglect. Students whose family life can be characterized as a life of privilege or entitlement (and/or the frequently accompanying life of indulgence) or as a life of emotional neglect (if not also financial or physical neglect) are most often the ones who do not make it through to a college degree. They are, in fact, the ones who most often encounter painful, emotional difficulties, some of which can lead to involvement of campus counselors and police.

The pitfalls for the privileged and sheltered

The two terms, privilege and neglect, represent the two extremes of the continuum with which most parents struggle: trying to be involved in their children's lives but not smothering them; trying to help, while getting out of the way at the same time. However, more is needed than to just find a happy medium between the two extremes; parents need to look at just what this means. What kind of parenting are we talking about?

Katie was a natural for an RA (resident assistant) position at Montana State University. Her mom, Caroline, described Katie as a "friend magnet" and very accepting of people, faults and all. Katie went through one and a half weeks of RA training, most of which concerned the programs and policies of the dorm and how to apply them for her dorm floor. But Katie came to the job already equipped with the most important tool she needed as an RA: she had been taught at home, long before her college years, to work out problems in a way that is acceptable to all parties involved. "People who don't do well in the dorm are people who haven't gotten over their stage of self-centeredness," Katie observed.

Katie explained that there was a group of four girls who came to her often to complain about each other and ask to be moved. Of the four, Katie said, "three were very spoiled and one was not." The girls were friends, but their friendship included a fair amount of drama that brought them knocking on Katie's door throughout the semester. They complained to Katie that they were not getting along and wanted to switch roommates. Katie and the four girls agreed to a swapped arrangement, but the complaints continued. One of the girls shifted rooms throughout the year and all of them, at one time or another, asked for a private room.

To make the situation worse, one of the girls Katie had described as "spoiled" began a hate campaign against another girl. After the victim asked for help, Katie agreed to talk with the perpetrator. As Katie described the victim's feelings, the initiator of the hate campaign argued that "her Nanna told her that she didn't have to be nice to somebody if she didn't want to be." Despite Katie's efforts to reason with the girl about her bullying, the girl continued her offensive behavior. "So the problem never got completely solved," Katie explained, "but I was able to get the rest of the girls on the floor to defend the victim and not join in on gossip and ridicule."

It seems apparent that at least some students who bully, including the student described above, are used to getting their own way more often than might be deemed healthy. Katie experienced and interpreted the situation as one in which a student's "stage of self-centeredness" has been unintentionally (or intentionally) nurtured during her younger years. The situation she described is typical of many students, in particular those described by counselors as rooted in the common problems of the entitled and indulged mentalities. Estranged roommates angrily demand to be moved immediately to another room, all the while asserting their claim that it was the other's behavior that caused the problem. Or conversely, a student isolates himself in his room in front of his computer and will not come out or talk with a counselor, choosing instead to stay perpetually "online."

Such behavior is evident in academics also. Every semester there are a few students who are blindsided by the fact that they are not getting the grades they received in high school.

Although the e-mail denouncing her teaching ability was anonymous, Dr. Williams was sure it came from Marie. Marie often skipped Dr. Williams's class and made little effort to discover what she might have missed. When Marie ended up with a failing grade on her midterm, she met with Dr. Williams to complain and insist that the grade was Dr. Williams's fault for being a poor teacher. Marie insisted she had made straight As in high school and that she would be making As now if the instruction were clear. Dr. Williams pointed out that Marie missed vital information when she skipped class and could not expect to perform well on tests. Marie finished the course with an F, and shortly afterward, Dr. Williams received an anonymous e-mail full of insults and highly critical comments about her teaching ability.

Like Marie, students who find themselves in academic trouble appear confused when discovering that they actually are going to be penalized for turning in a research paper a week late. They express dismay, and even outrage, that an argument with their roommate the night before a test does not automatically earn them the right to take a makeup exam. Parking tickets have to be paid, not ignored; property damage resulting from a party is the host's responsibility, even if the guests were uninvited. Add to this the normal pressures of final exams, and what often happens is that these same students engage in angry, acting-out behaviors that may include excessive drinking or drugging, fighting, or vandalism. One campus police official, when asked what would be the first message he wished to convey to parents, stated emphatically that parents need to have established a lifestyle of "structure and consequences" for their children long before coming to college.

Probably every child today has experienced a "time-out" or some other form of discipline for pushing, shoving, not sharing, temper tantrums, or whatever. The problem is, once our kids are teenagers, many of us either neglect to follow through in imposing such consequences or else we are inconsistent about it, often backing down under a barrage of teenage logic. In reality, consequences are much more difficult to impose and enforce once our children reach that sudden argumentative and defiant stage of adolescence so well depicted in the popular comic strip "Zits." Author Anthony Wolf speaks directly about the difficulty of parenting teenagers in his book, *Get Out of My Life, but first could you drive me and Cheryl to the mall?*:

> *Teenagers of today have been raised in an era of far less harsh parenting practices. Their world may be complicated and scary; nonetheless, they feel more empowered than teenagers of previous generations. They are mouthier, less directly obedient, especially at home. This change in teenager behavior is real. It requires a similar change in teenager parenting.*

While we struggle to find the parenting technique to fit the problem at hand, the effort becomes confusing if the consequences come from someone else, such as a teacher or the soccer coach. We may instinctively jump to our child's defense without looking into the situation more closely. It is possible, after all, that our Josh or Sarah did, in fact, strike the first blow, cheat on a test, or scream at the referee. As difficult as it may be to accept, while our children are on that proverbial road to maturity, it is important for them to occasionally push the boundaries a little and check out the result. Such behavior is not only normal, but essential if kids are going to figure out how the world really works. But it also is important that there be parentally imposed consequences while they are still under our care; otherwise, they will push further until other authorities, such as school staff or law enforcement, do the enforcing.

We need to remember that if and when our legal-adult students go off to college, we will not be there to rescue or protect them, nor will we be there to administer consequences, and we shouldn't be. Josh and Sarah will be required to function as adults, without a parent's watchful eye and steadying hand. This is not to say, however, that they should be or will be cut loose with no emotional or financial support (see Chapters 8 and 9). What it does mean is that if we've been running interference for our kids throughout middle and high school—arguing with their teachers over grades or requirements, helping them put a project together the night before it is due, pulling them from an activity because they do not immediately excel, making excuses for them when they miss a homework assignment— then we should not be surprised if they find the adjustment to college life extremely difficult, even overwhelming. Peter Stearns of George Mason University and author of *Anxious Parenting: A History of Modern Childrearing in America*, says that parents often don't believe their child can handle a difficult situation. "Middle-class parents especially assume that if kids start getting into difficulty they need to rush in and do it for them, rather than let them flounder a bit and learn from it. I don't mean we should abandon them," Stearns said, "but give them more credit for figuring things out." As child psychologist and Tufts University professor David Elkind says in the 2004 article "A Nation of Wimps": "Kids need to feel badly sometimes. We learn through experience and we learn through bad experiences. Through failure, we learn how to cope."

If you see yourself as a parent who has perhaps been rescuing, try this approach the next time your high schooler comes crying over a missed assignment: "It sounds like you've got a problem. What are you going to do about it?" Then, let your student do the doing. Many times students get it right, as the following story illustrates.

> Serena chose Colorado State University because she wanted to experience a part of the country outside her native California. Serena admits she was lucky to have supportive parents who were always willing to listen. It also helped that her parents were wealthy and could afford to pay for her to have a single room in the dorm after she and her roommate became unbearable to each other. They also paid for a cell phone plan with 5,000 unlimited minutes, they flew out to see her a few times each school year, and they shipped Serena's two horses to

Colorado. "I was sheltered and very lucky," Serena said of her family life. But her parents expected Serena to be serious about her schoolwork and to work for her spending money. She did both, working part-time, landing an internship, and graduating with a degree in communications. Best of all, she is well adjusted and ready to face the world.

Resisting the urge to shelter, to rush in and do it yourself, to fix it when something goes wrong, is hard for many parents. But letting your teenager do it himself, make mistakes, and face consequences gives him the experiences and skills that will help him as he ventures off after high school.

The pitfalls of neglect

The other end of the family environment continuum is neglect. There have always been, and continue to be, parents who take the attitude, "You're on your own now. You're eighteen years old and out of the house; whatever happens you'll have to deal with it." While it is true that some students can cope with this situation, and even excel under these circumstances, it is generally a mistake to think that your son or daughter is one of those who can. Students whose parents do not call or write, do not visit the campus or their student's dorm or apartment, or do not become involved when the student receives some form of disciplinary action or begins failing classes—these are the students who often disappear off the university radar screen pretty quickly. Many never return.

Although the movie "Ordinary People" is dated, some of its themes still seem to resonate with students. After viewing a portion of the movie (in a class on family dynamics), including scenes in which severe communication problems between the troubled son and his mother are portrayed, a student approached her instructor after class. "That's my family they were showing," she said. "I'm so alone." In the same class, another student wrote in his journal: "My dad and mom are divorced, and my dad has decided that buying a motorcycle and touring the country is more important than my college education, both financially and in terms of him calling me or coming to see me. He says that it's his turn now."

It should be noted that all forms of neglect are not relatively easy to recognize. In reality, neglect can be completely unintentional. There are many parents who, even while they may be wringing their hands and frantically trying to figure out what to do about their student who shows signs of being lost, depressed, or unable to cope, may be so intimidated by the prospect of interfering that they become immobilized.

By the time kids are in their late teens and are preparing to leave high school, parents have been repeatedly advised to "let loose" and allow their fledglings to learn from their own experiences. Paradoxically, however, if taken to extreme, this otherwise sound advice can become the cause of serious problems if it results in our failure to act on our student's interest when that help is most needed.

Jim Weber, M.S.W., therapist and counselor at Colorado State University, works with students who are facing disciplinary action by the university. He described the common situation of a student running out of options: The old coping strategies from high school are not working, grades are falling, money is tight, and disciplinary action is pending, perhaps not for the first time. In spite of a certain amount of "I'm fine, nothing to worry about" posturing on the part of the student, Weber said this is the time it is crucial for parents to be the older, wiser, and supportive adult family member. "I wish I could empower parents more, to get them involved more directly," Weber said. "Too many are timid about trying to intercede when their son or daughter show signs of trouble." The student, Weber said, has been so successful in getting her parents to "back off" that she cannot easily turn back to the parents for help, and the parents are uncomfortable taking the initiative.

Weber, as well as other counselors who concurred with his view, reported that parents of students who are seriously struggling sometimes call university counselors to talk about their student's situation—be it pending academic suspension or substance abuse problems or roommate issues. While these parents are clearly worried about their son or daughter, they are often reluctant to talk with the students themselves, either over the phone or in person. Counselors said that a common parental response is: "I don't want to be too doting or interfering."

Add to this the privacy and confidentially laws that prohibit counselors or other staff from revealing any specifics concerning the nature of a student's situation, and you end up with parents asking counselors to act as intermediaries—something they cannot do. What they can and often will do is recommend that parents contact the student directly, and they encourage students to talk with their parents. From the counselors' viewpoint, when a student is failing or moving into a substance abuse problem or is otherwise overwhelmed, that is when parents need to be involved even if the student does not want to admit that he needs help. Of course, families with a history of talking to each other frequently and openly, even during those difficult teen years of high school, are going to be the best prepared.

Paulo, a University of Florida architecture student, believes parents should not "baby" kids while they are in high school. He adjusted well to college life, primarily, he said, because his parents made him responsible for curfews and other social issues while he was in high school; abuse of those responsibilities came with reasonable consequences. Some of his new college friends were not so lucky. Paulo told the story of a "preacher's daughter" who had been raised in a very strict, parent-controlled environment. "She couldn't handle the freedom when she got to college," Paulo recalls. During her first semester she began drinking regularly and became sexually active with more than one member of the football team. Her parents discovered her inappropriate, risky behavior, yanked her out of the university, and enrolled her in a small school near their home. "They were a great family, but her father was more involved in his work than his kids," Paulo said. "When she moved to the University of Florida, she went wild."

Intervention when a student is in trouble is not the kind of involvement that constitutes a parent trying to rescue a student from the consequences of her actions. Rather, older adults—parents, counselors, and other relevant participants—are trying to constructively help the student deal with whatever consequences she already faces so that she can recover and move on. Options are created, new choices made. It also should be noted that in a few such cases, if the relationship between parent and student involves abuse or other dysfunctional dynamics, the counselors might recommend a course of action to the student that represents a positive intervention strategy but does not rely on direct parental involvement.

Preparing Your Teenager: Growing Your Teenager's Maturity

So, how do we help our teenagers be "ready"? At this point, two basic facts stand out: First, the emotional maturity necessary to steer through the college years will not develop mysteriously during the last few months of high school—they must be developed during the early and midteen years. Second, you and your student have choices. You have choices about when, where, and under what circumstances college comes into the picture, or if, in fact, it comes into the picture at all. The following scenarios offer suggestions to consider as you prepare your students for the challenges

and changes they will face when they make the transition to college life.
1) Make a list of your teenager's emotional strengths and weaknesses, as in
the following example:

Strengths	Weaknesses
Shows bravery by participating in new events without friends.	Doesn't follow through on what he promises.
Probes until he gets an answer he understands.	Has a hot temper and is argumentative.
Is friendly and outgoing.	Is anxious if left out.
Is able to recognize when he is wrong and apologize.	Takes too many risks at weekend parties.

2) Encourage and reward your student's strengths.

Challenge	Solution
Your teenager decides to play on a city recreation soccer team after failing to make the high school team.	Praise her for continuing to play a sport she enjoys just for the fun of it. Show up for the rec games and support her team.
Although she really wants to go to a friend's party, your teenager accepts that she must attend a family event instead.	Praise her for seeing the importance of family as well as friends, and be sure that other family members engage her warmly. Suggest she host a party for her friends in the near future.
Without prompting, your teenager tells you she lied about where she was. She apologizes and admits she did wrong.	Explain that although you are disappointed in her lying, you accept the apology sincerely and you are glad she realizes it was wrong. Ask her why she lied and why she apologized. Work through the process with her to reinforce good decision making.

3) Develop a lifestyle of structure and consequences for your teenager.

Challenge	Solution
More than once, your teenager has agreed to feed and exercise the neighbors' dog while they are out of town. He consistently has a conflict and begs you to feed the dog in his place.	You should refuse the first time it happens, but if you have covered for him a few times, stop doing so. If he is away from home at feeding time, charge him for the inconvenience of picking him up to bring him home to feed the dog or charge him for feeding the dog yourself. Or, make him explain to the neighbor that he asked you to feed however many times and be sure the neighbor reduces his payment for the times you fed their dog.
Your teenager asks if he can borrow the car to meet some friends at the movie. He is a newly licensed driver and is not allowed to have passengers yet. You discover he took two friends to the movie.	Before your teenager is granted a driver's license, have a signed driving contract that clearly spells out your expectations and consequences for infractions. Be sure you state that driving is a privilege, not a right. Example contracts are readily available on the Internet. Confront him and ask him for an explanation. Listen without interruption, then ask him to repeat the law (or your rules) about passengers for new drivers. Pull out the contract and show him the consequence already agreed upon. Most important, follow through on those consequences.

Challenge	Solution
Your teenager tells you he is spending the night with a friend, but instead goes to an unsupervised party, where he spends the night. You find out when talking to the friend's parents	Confront your teenager with the evidence. Ask him to explain his actions and why he lied, then listen. Remind him of your expectations and why you didn't want him to go, then ask him what he thinks should happen as a result of his behavior—he might give you some good ideas! Carry through on whatever consequences you implement.

4) Help your teenager find common ground and reach satisfactory conclusions during conflict.

Challenge	Solution
Your teenager explodes in anger if you tell her she cannot attend a certain party.	You know the mantra here: Don't get caught in the escalation. As hard as it is to do, you should firmly state that there will be no discussion until she calms down, then walk away. When she (and you) calm down, acknowledge her efforts to try again. Listen to her arguments for the party without interruption, be open-minded, and look for information you might have missed. Then insist she listen to your arguments against the party without interruption. If she explodes again, start over. If not, ask her if she can think of a compromise. Have one in mind yourself. Although you have the ultimate decision, the point is to try to teach her to handle conflict without exploding and to work toward a satisfactory conclusion.

Challenge	Solution
Your teenager tells you that a group of friends she hangs with has started putting down and trying to embarrass a girl that your daughter has known since preschool; the girl is shy and a loner. Your daughter feels uncomfortable but wants to stay in favor with the popular girls.	First listen to her dilemma. Then ask her why she thinks the popular girls are after the shy girl. Ask her how she thinks the shy girl feels about the way she is treated. Ask her if she has ever felt that way. Ask her if she feels confident enough to tell the popular girls to stop their bullying. What will she lose? If she doesn't feel strong enough, suggest that she walk away when the bullying begins. Then ask her to be sure to talk with the shy girl, maybe asking her to get together for a movie or a sleepover. Keep the conversation going over the following days, trying to build your teen's self-confidence enough to say no to the bullying.
Your teenager comes home in a rage, calling her math teacher foul names and claiming he is out to get her. You know she struggles in math and the teacher has a reputation of being tough. She begs you to call the school and have her switched to another class or she knows she will fail.	Begin by telling her you will talk with her after she has a chance to calm down. Then ask her about the difficulties she is having in class— focus on the academics, not the teacher. Ask what help she has asked for. If the answer is none, suggest she start by talking with her teacher. Remind her that there will always be teachers, and future employers, whom she will not like. Nevertheless, it is crucial to learn to work with all kinds of people. Follow up in the following days to see if she has spoken with her teacher.

5) Guide your teenager toward coping skills to overcome his shortcomings.

Challenge	Solution
Your teenager is shy and doesn't like to speak out or ask questions in class. He must take a speech class to fulfill district graduation requirements.	Recognize that a speech class will be tough for your son. At family events or social activities, ask a few adults to go out of their way to ask him questions about what he is doing or his plans, carrying on a genuine conversation. Take your son to hear speakers, particularly those telling a story of overcoming hardships. Encourage your son to participate in organizations that allow opportunities to speak up and be involved, such as Scouts or 4-H. Relate your personal stories of overcoming a hardship. Praise his efforts at speaking up.
Your teenager is a good student, but he lacks confidence and follows after the popular crowd instead of finding his own way. More than once you have found out he was drinking while "hanging" with the crowd.	While the dangers and illegality of drinking, and consequences for imbibing, should be part of the conversation, you also should ask how he feels about his behavior. Ask him to repeat the rules and laws about underage drinking. Ask him how he feels about breaking those laws. Help him to identify safe, but peer-approved, activities in which he can participate. Suggest he plan some of those events and ask friends to join him. Steer him toward activities he feels good about and in which he can take a lead.

6) Give your teenager the opportunity to learn from her mistakes.

Challenge	Solution
The big history project was assigned a month earlier. Your teenager waited until the weekend before the Monday it was due to get started. It was clear to her by Sunday afternoon that she was not going to complete it on time. She begs you to let her stay home on Monday to finish, claiming she'll never let something go this late again.	You are tempted to let her stay home because you know it will hurt her grade if she doesn't turn the project in on time. However, she most likely will let something go this late again if she sees you will cover for her. Tell her you are sorry she waited so long, but that she must face the consequences of procrastinating. Follow up to be sure she does finish the project.
A player on the opposing team shoves and trips other players without the referee's notice. In anger, your teenager strikes out and trips the player in full sight of the referee. She argues with the referee and is carded. Her coach suspends her from the next game. Still angry at home, she swears she will quit.	Tell her you want to talk with her after she calms down. Go over what happened in the game, acknowledging the unfairness of the opposing player. Then ask her what she gained by taking revenge. What did it do for her team? Did it punish the offending player? Ask her what would have been a better response in the game. Ask her if she thinks a referee has ever made a mistake in her favor. Suggest she apologize to her coach and the offending player.

7) Practice intervention, not interference.

Challenge	Solution
Your teenager has stopped doing his homework. His grades and behavior are slipping. He is a bright young man with lots of potential. A couple of times you have called a teacher, made excuses, and threatened him into finishing a homework assignment.	Stop making excuses. Ask him why he has let his schoolwork slide. Try to keep an open conversation and listen to what he says. Set up a meeting with teachers and ask how he is doing in class. Is he participating? Is he disruptive? Listen to what suggestions the teacher may offer. Who is he "hanging" with? What do he and his friends do? If you suspect your teenager may be experiencing anxiety or depression, seek the help of a professional. Decide if you want to set up consequences, such as loss of driving privileges or activities, but be prepared that it may not work and accept that he must pay the penalty for neglecting his schoolwork.
Your teenager has the habit of not starting what he finishes. He signs up for a recreation sport but drops out by midseason; you call the coach and make excuses. He angers his school project teammates because he never does his share; you end up doing his part. He signs up for Scout or youth group trips and half the time ends up pulling out; you make his excuses.	Stop covering for your teenager. He needs to take responsibility for his commitments. Make it clear that the next event he signs up for, he must follow through to completion. Consider making him earn at least part of the money to sign up for a sports team or to participate in an organization's trip. If he wants to quit, tell him he must talk to the coach or the trip leader and explain fully why he is backing out. At that point, he should assume full financial loss for the activity. Refuse to complete his part in school group projects. Let his project mates, and the teacher, do the punishing.

Challenge	Solution
You find evidence of marijuana in your teenager's backpack. One of his friends' parents hints that your son has been drinking at parties. You feel out of control and don't know what to do	This is a definite time for intervention; if you do nothing, he may believe you don't care. While many teenagers experiment with drugs and alcohol, your teenager also may feel out of control and truly need a "heavy hand" to back out of his situation. Confiscate the evidence and confront your teenager. Instead of lecturing, ask him what the laws are and what dangers he places himself in when he chooses to imbibe. Ask him if he knows what will happen if he is arrested by the police. Ask him what consequences he thinks are appropriate and seriously consider them, but have specific consequences ready.

Remember that success in college involves much more than just academic preparedness. During your teenager's high school years, look for gaps in her maturity. Keep the communication channels open and analyze poor decisions while praising good ones. Don't make excuses for your teenager, but let her learn from her mistakes. Provide opportunities where she can talk to adults and grow confident in discussing her ideas. Model compromise and planning, and help her find that path to success.

Chapter 2

Going to College Now, Later, or Never?
Is Your Teenager Willing?

You want your teenager to go to college. You believe that a college education offers the best chances for a career that will provide your son or daughter with a good quality of life. But what does your student want and believe? You assume that your teenager understands your perspective and is onboard with the college track, but are you sure? Despite the fact that your teenager may realize that college does offer the best opportunity, that doesn't mean she actually wants to go straight out of high school. She may want to go later, or she may choose a different route entirely. It is time to start listening to, and seriously considering, her ideas and dreams.

Who owns the idea of going to college?

Much has been written and said in recent years about the idea that people need a sense of ownership when it comes to major issues in their lives. Although this may be an overused idea, when it comes to teenagers' feelings about going on to college after high school, parents need to pay attention.

Megan had wanted to be a hairstylist since she was fourteen years old. For Megan, being a hairstylist combined the things she enjoyed most: working with people and being creative in a real hands-on kind of way—like sculpting, but much more friendly and social. Her closet drawers were full of magazines about styling techniques and trends; she did her friends' hair whenever she got the chance; and on her own, she had even researched the schools near her hometown and checked into possible financial aid. However, for her mother, Susan, hairstyling school was not an option she would consider for her daughter. A divorced single parent, Susan had struggled to keep herself and her two children going for ten long years. Daily she was grateful for her college degree and teaching credentials, without which she was certain they would never have made it. Regardless of any ideas Megan had to the contrary, Susan felt that her duty as a parent was to make sure that her kids had college educations.

Megan spent four miserable years in college, generally slipping by with minimal grades except in the four art classes she took. Over time, her self-esteem began to suffer noticeably, and her choices in her social life shifted also. She found herself drawn to other students who were unhappy or just generally cynical about school, spending more and more of her time away from school and the people she associated with it. By the end of her senior year, she was barely passing her required courses and beginning to drink heavily. She even posed as her mother over the phone to the registrar's office in an attempt to get a grade changed. She did not attend graduation.

Three years later Megan was married and had two children. After completing her degree, she attended night school to become a hairstylist and worked days at a local hardware store. She does consider that some day her college degree might provide a safety net, and she admitted that it could someday be a lifesaver for her and her young family. She also said that her four years of college were a waste, and that if she had followed her own dream, she could have had her own salon by now.

It is apparent that Megan did not "own" the idea of going to college. Megan needed, as do all our children, to hear support of her right to self-determination, instead of nonsupportive comments such as, "You won't be able to do anything useful or interesting without a college degree," or,

"You won't ever make any money with a degree in music, and I won't pay for it if that's what you decide to do."

If this is the stance parents repeatedly take with their eighteen-year-old or nineteen-year-old adult child, then these parents should not be surprised when their son or daughter decides to stop studying, stop going to class, stop calling home, or even move without informing Mom or Dad. Each semester, on every campus, there are students who disappear, who may or may not bother to withdraw officially, and whom university staff may or may not know anything about. While students are all individuals with their own unique circumstances, in many of these cases a contributing factor is a lack of ownership. To them the idea of college, with all the emotional, social, and academic adjustments that are required, is something imposed on them by somebody else, and they resent it.

As was expected of her, Brittany entered the University of Maryland right after high school. She was a bright girl and expected to do well in school—which she did. She did not, however, return the next year. "There wasn't anything wrong," Brittany explained. "I just think that I didn't want to go in the first place. I didn't like the idea that people had a notion of what college should be for me, and what I should get out of it." Brittany had not declared a major as a freshman, something she said made her feel as if school had no purpose. "I was looking for a reason for spending all that money and time out of my life," she said. "It was fun, but I had hoped I would figure out what I wanted to be when I grew up."

Brittany said she had to convince her parents that she needed the time off, but once she explained it to them, they were supportive. "It introduced them to the concept of me making my own decisions—and the world didn't come to an end," Brittany mused.

After working a year as a kindergarten aide, Brittany returned to school and graduated with a degree in history. Brittany still says she does not know what she wants to do with her life. "That doesn't bother me as much anymore," she said, primarily because she chose her own path. She is now doing a stint with AmeriCorps, hoping to gain insight on what to do next.

Taking time off after high school

Taking responsibility for their decisions is a dramatic step for teenagers, as Brittany demonstrated. Add the stress of figuring out what you want to be when you grow up loads the pressure. It is important to give young people time to think and decide about their futures.

Gap Year

Taking time to think about what the future holds may include a year or two off school, in which the young adult gets a job, travels, or engages in a structured "gap year." A gap year is a period of time between the end of secondary school and college, or between college years, in which students enroll in a structured program that gives them the opportunity to travel, work, or volunteer at home or internationally. The gap year concept was born in England as a way to fill time in between students' taking their "A" levels (that is, university entrance exams) and the time when their studies began. British universities encourage the in-between students to explore their interests, see the world, or just do something productive during the gap. Statistics from the United Kingdom show a steady increase in the number of students taking a gap year, and the idea is catching on in the United States. Some colleges and universities—University of Chicago, Massachusetts Institute of Technology, and Harvard, to name a few—will defer enrollment for one year if a student is enrolled in a structured gap year and agrees not to apply to another university. One gap year program, Dynamy, is a U.S. nonprofit experiential education organization that offers mentored internships, urban and wilderness leadership opportunities, career advising, and independent living. Dynamy is a pricey program, as are most gap year programs, but AmeriCorps, for example, is much less expensive and offers challenging local, state, or national community service to meet U.S. educational, public safety, health, and environmental needs. A bonus of AmeriCorps is that full-time volunteers are eligible for monetary education awards to pay for college. There are hundreds of gap year programs—it would be time well spent for interested students and parents to browse the Internet for ideas.

As Phil neared the end of high school, he felt overwhelming pressure about college. Phil said that because he lived near Boston there was excessive hype about going to private or Ivy League schools. Phil became depressed and burdened about attending the "right" school. He knew he would have a hard time because his grades weren't up to Ivy League standards, so he decided to delay—to take a gap year.

His parents were supportive; however, they wanted to know how he would fill the time. Phil was already working on a personal film documentary project, and he definitely wanted to continue that work. To support himself, Phil lived at home and worked as a waiter in a nearby restaurant. Occasionally, acquaintances would come into the restaurant and ask Phil what he was doing. Phil said that he always got the cold shoulder when he replied that he was "just working."

Eventually Phil's parents convinced him to try some other things during his gap year—specifically international volunteer work. After searching the Internet for a program, Phil ended up with seven other young volunteers in a daycare program for the elderly just outside Lima, Peru. "The elderly walked to the center and we fed them two good meals a day," Phil explained. "Then we'd spend a few hours in the afternoon doing arts and crafts and just talking." The talking boosted Phil's Spanish-speaking abilities.

After five months in Peru, Phil and some friends traveled to central China where he volunteered for a month in a center for developmentally disabled children. After that stint, Phil and friends traveled through more of China, then through Tibet and Nepal.

Phil now feels ready to start school at Goucher College in Maryland. He hopes to major in film with a minor in international studies. Having shared cramped quarters in Peru and China, Phil is certain he won't have any problems with dorm life.

Phil's father, Robert, confirmed that Phil was truly on his own in Peru and China. Phil had to figure out his finances, how to get around, and how to communicate. He learned a great deal, Robert said, and most important, he matured into a more confident and capable young man. "The changes in Phil during this past year are stunning," Robert said. Robert shares Phil's certainty that Phil is now ready, willing, and able to succeed in college and beyond.

Working toward school

Fortunately for Phil, his parents supported his delayed, yet fruitful, path to college. Many students and parents, however, find out the hard way that college, right out of high school, might not be the best choice. The need for the student to see school as a necessary step toward achieving his own goals, not those of his parents or even his closest friends, is described by parents, students, and administrators as a key factor in whether or not a student sticks it out and, in the end, succeeds in achieving an education that connects him or her to a meaningful career.

Jerome, a C-average student, left college after two unhappy semesters at two different schools, worked construction jobs for a year with two of his friends, then returned to school and successfully completed his degree program at age twenty-three. As he described it, his two major problems had been that (1) he had only attended college originally because it was expected of him, and (2) he needed time off to discover what he wanted to do. A year of staring at the TV every night and drinking beer while not saving any money helped as well.

Parents often fear that their student will not return to college if he or she takes time off as Jerome did. While it is true that some students do not return after leaving college midstream, it is also true that many return, invigorated, matured, and serious about their schoolwork. Over and over again faculty report that nontraditional students, generally defined as twenty-five years or older, who have been in the labor market for a while and then return to school are typically much more motivated than the average student coming straight from high school, are also generally more mature, and bring with them the experiences and skills they have attained outside the school environment. These are often the students who most visibly contribute to classroom discussions and end up with better grades than their younger, traditional student classmates.

Jack said his high school years were tough. He is dyslexic and that made schoolwork difficult. He graduated as a middle-of-the-road student and swore he was done with school forever.

At eighteen, Jack went to work in construction, first sweeping floors and doing final cleanups, but eventually working his way up. After thirteen years of the hard physical work, Jack looked at the workers around him and decided he didn't want to be forty-plus years old with ailments caused by the hard work involved in construction. "Plus, I was bored and wanted more stability," Jack said.

At age thirty-one, Jack enrolled at Colorado State University on academic probationary status. His first semester, Jack earned five As and one B, and four years later he graduated with honors in industrial science and technology education. He went on to receive a master's degree in manufacturing technology and construction management, attaining a 3.98 GPA. As an undergraduate, Jack was the campus president of the Society of Industrial Technology Education and a national vice president of the Technology Education Collegiate Association. He was involved, serious, and focused, and he brought real experience to the classroom. He now teaches technology education in a junior high school, a job he truly enjoys.

Despite a several years' delay between high school and college, Jack's route proved successful.

College is not for everyone

While parents should stay open to the idea of a gap year—or gap years—there are other things they can do in advance of college to help their student with the overwhelming possibilities in the world. Most senior high and middle schools (and many elementary schools) have programs designed to introduce various occupational choices to kids. Community adults working in a variety of fields, whether in firefighting, medicine, hotel management, or computer programming, visit schools and give presentations. Our country promotes a national "Take Your Daughter to Work Day," which in some areas has been expanded to include boys as well. Teachers in English classes across the country often require essays on a career of the student's choice, possibly based on an interview with an adult working in that field. Some high schools require a semester-long course, usually in the freshman or sophomore year, which takes students through the process of writing resumes, applying for jobs, and "shadowing" an adult in his or her work. In nearly every such case, the student is asked to focus on the educational requirements involved for a particular profession or field of work.

Why is it, then, that some high school graduates who come to college don't really seem to want to be there? Why is it that they seem to have so little motivation? One of the most common complaints among faculty is the "time clock" mentality, the impression that some students are simply putting in their time, much as one does when working at a job that is of no interest. There is an apparent lack of enthusiasm for not only the specific subject matter (understandable, as not everyone is going to love algebra), but also for school in general. Parents should consider their child's attitude about school long before they plunk down a few thousand dollars at the college registration desk.

Like his brother before him, Salman went straight into college after graduating from high school. Unlike his brother, Salman wasn't ready. After his first semester at the University of West Virginia, Salman was placed on academic probation. Although he had promised Mom and Dad he would work harder, he did little better the second semester. Once home, he sincerely apologized to his parents for wasting their money, said he would find a job, and told them he would not return to school, anywhere, in the fall. His mom said that although it was hard to accept, she respects Salman's realization that he is not ready for college now—and possibly may never be.

Although Salman's decision to drop out was difficult for his parents to accept, they realized they could not force him to succeed in school. Letting him find his own way will ultimately prove the better path, as Carlos shows in the following story.

Diagnosed with dyslexia in junior high school, Carlos had always struggled with academics. However, he wanted to try college, so he joined his brother at Texas A&M University. He was on academic probation after the first semester, and for the second semester he decided to try a few courses at a community college rather than continuing at A&M. Over a period of three years, Carlos took a few courses at different community colleges as he moved locations, all the while working at various jobs. After he had moved near Dallas, Carlos landed a job with a lighting company. He helped with deliveries, and before long he was helping with installations. The company already considered Carlos a good, dependable worker, and one day they suggested he apply for an electrician's apprenticeship position. Carlos jumped at the chance. He is now leading his apprenticeship class, loves the work, and is looking forward to a career as a master electrician.

As Carlos' story illustrates, there are other commendable paths to success and a career besides college. Parents need to contemplate those other options and let their child choose the path that is best for him or her; the following story is yet another example.

As her senior year in high school closed in, Abby contemplated a career in forensic science. She enrolled in a local community college but did not like it. "I should have known then that I just didn't like going to school," Abby said. "I just wanted to learn the things I needed, not all the basic courses you have to take."

Still, Abby's mom convinced her to try a university in the hope that Abby might like it better. She completed one semester at the University of North Texas, then dropped out.

Focusing on what she liked, working with makeup and skin care, Abby next enrolled in a cosmetology school. "By the end of the first week, I absolutely loved it," Abby said. She graduated early and passed her state license exam. Still searching for a more specific field, Abby learned of a cosmetology graduate school, the International Dermal Institute. There, Abby could focus on skin care and earn the title of esthetician. Abby is currently working toward the required one hundred hours of classes and seminars needed to gain a post-cosmetology graduate diploma. As she loved cosmetology school, Abby loves the specialized classes she now takes. Best of all, she is working as a receptionist in a salon whose owner has promised to hire her as an esthetician after she receives her diploma.

Salman's, Carlos' and Abby's stories illustrate that forcing your teenager into college without any consideration for his or her wishes is usually a waste of time and money if the student has little to no interest in schoolwork. Consider that the vast majority of college classes require performance on tests and papers only, and these may be few and far between. College requires a considerable level of self-motivation to show up when no one is keeping track, perhaps to an early morning class in a subject you dislike, so that four months in the future you will receive a good grade. Rarely will a teacher take attendance, rarely will a teacher inquire about a missing grade until the end of the term, and, particularly in the case of large introductory classes, it is a rare teacher indeed who will know your student's name unless the student makes a point of introducing herself. If going to class is your idea, not hers, it is highly probable that your student will not maintain the effort.

Careers with or without college

The earlier revelations about parents who refuse to financially support their students unless they pick the right major or who refuse to consider their student's choice to pursue something other than college were not fabricated. Students talking with academic advisors and mental health counselors often describe this type of conflict with parents. Some students have admitted, or sometimes even boasted, that they are taking classes their parents do not even know about, secretly pursuing their own major while neglecting the one favored by Mom and Dad. Although it is true that such students usually are motivated in their course work, they can easily end up needing an extra year or more to graduate since they have been pursuing two majors. It is beyond the scope of this book to delve into all of the implications of these conflicts at length, but there are a couple of important points to consider.

First, the choices you and your student make about entering college now or a few years from now, or about picking a major, are not immutable. After all, the average adult in the United States changes occupations five times, proving that few of us pick a career and hang on steadily for forty years or more. Add to that the fact that many employers are looking only for the degree itself as an indication of basic skill levels and maturity, often with the assumption that the employer will be providing actual job training, and the specific academic major one selects seems less crucial. Nearly all degree programs include a core of basic classes for all students—generally two to four semesters' worth—so your student will have time to look into interesting possibilities while sampling a range of subject areas. Even students majoring in areas such as the social sciences or humanities, which many consider employment wastelands, actually tend to do quite well in the labor market. For example, as reported in *The College Majors Handbook: The Actual Jobs, Earnings, and Trends for Graduates of 60 College Majors*, social science majors with a bachelor's degree registered a labor force participation rate of 84.1 percent, and those in the humanities registered a rate of 77.5 percent. In humanities, students earning a master's degree increased that rate significantly to 83.3 percent.

Second, one of the options available is for your student to forgo college, either now or possibly forever. For example, in Megan's case cited earlier, had the same investment in time and money spent for attaining the college degree been invested in attaining beautician certification, it might have paid off just as well or better. When asked, employment counselors can point to various fields in which people without college degrees can and do earn highly respectable wages and enjoy significant job security. Michael Farr, in his *Best Jobs for the 21st Century*, lists several careers that do not necessarily require college degrees, but do require on-the-job training from between a few weeks to four years. Among those jobs listed with the best salaries are truck drivers, refractory materials repairers, sales representatives, subway and streetcar operators, crane and tower operators, police officers, electricians, environmental compliance inspectors, inspectors and investigators of numerous industries, air traffic controllers, elevator installers and repairers, fire fighting and prevention supervisors, telecommunications facility examiners, insurance appraisers, and millwrights.

Remember that the choices you and your student make need to reflect your student's needs, qualities, and interests—not his best friend's, not her sister's or brother's, and not yours. He is the one who will need to do the work, and she is the one who will need to feel motivated to do so. The good thing, for both students and parents, is that we live in a society with myriad possible careers and possible schools (including those that are not colleges) from which to pick. So, if Megan wants beautician's training and her sister Emily wants a degree in accounting, so be it. Same for Tom, who dreams of avalanche control work in Montana while brother Sean has his sights set on law school.

Preparing Your Teenager:
Exploring Options for the Future

Explore the various paths to college with your teenagers. Help them make a realistic plan for success and give them opportunities to explore their ideas.

1) Listen to your teenager's ideas about life after high school.

Challenge	Solution
During his junior year, you drag your teenager to all the college informational meetings offered by his high school. You eagerly tell him about your favorite colleges and talk about how exciting it will be for him. He finally tells you he is not sure he wants to go to college, at least not right away.	Take a deep breath, then listen to what he says. Find out what his concerns are, if he has a plan, and what he sees as a path toward that plan. If no plan exists (and often it doesn't), help him start one. Help him consider all his options: working, a gap year, a couple of community college classes, technical training, the military, etc. Have him speak with his school counselor for ideas. Ask him to consider applying to one or two colleges in case he changes his mind. Keep the conversation going throughout the rest of high school until he finds something that satisfies him, and, hopefully, you also.
Your high school student hates school and has told you repeatedly that he will not go to college.	Remember that this is his decision. Forcing him to go to college will be costly and, most likely, ineffective. Ask him what he does want to do, then help him make a plan as described above. Include in that planning the financial responsibilities he will incur after leaving high school. If this is difficult for you, remember that he might change his mind in a few years.

Challenge	Solution
Your teenager says he wants to go to college, but he wants a chance to be on his own and earn some money first.	Praise him for having a plan. Help him look at work options. Does he want to work in his local community? Has he considered a technical job that requires some training and offers him specific skills? Does he have a time frame as to when he wants to apply to college?
Your teenager is smart, witty, and capable, and she makes good grades, but she's bored with school. She tells you she doesn't want to go to college right after high school.	It is a positive step for your teenager to recognize that she isn't ready for college yet. Start working with her now to come up with a plan for the intervening years. Does she want to work and save some money? Does she want to volunteer with an organization such as AmeriCorps or an overseas organization? Ask her to consider applying to colleges in case she changes her mind. Be clear on your expectations of her during the intervening years: Is she on her own for expenses? Will you loan her money? Can she live at home? Help her plot a path to success.

Challenge	Solution
Your high school junior coasts through school, content with average grades. He doesn't assert himself, but follows the crowd and often makes poor and/or dangerous decisions. He tells everyone he plans to go to college right after high school, but you don't think he is ready.	Start conversations now about the expectations and expense of college. Have him talk with school counselors, check out Web sites, and talk with college students to fully understand what he will face in college. Suggest that he consider taking a class or two at a community college before deciding if he wants to commit to a four-year university. Explore options other than going immediately to college. Find that path to success.

2) Consider a gap year.

Challenge	Solution
Your teenager makes good grades but is easily distracted, bored, and uninspired. She says she wants to go to college, but she also says she doesn't want to look at schools and really doesn't care where she goes. You don't think she is ready for college.	Agree with her that college is a good idea, but add that she doesn't have to go right after high school. Ask her what she thinks of taking some time off—a gap year—to think about what she really wants. Research organized gap year programs or try to set something up yourself through personal connections. Listen to her ideas and together find a program or idea that excites her and will give her the opportunity to grow and learn.

Challenge	Solution
Your teenager wants to take a year off before college, but she has her heart set on one or two colleges.	Be supportive of her knowing she wants a year off before college. Have her research her college choices to determine if they will defer enrollment. Research her gap year options and come up with a program that works with the college of her choice.

3) Work with your teenager to choose the best path for him.

Challenge	Solution
Your teenager wants to go to college but has no ideas for a major or a career.	Together, make a list of his interests and look for opportunities to expose your teenager to various jobs. Take him to career fairs offered at his high school or in the community. Find out if his school offers a course that allows students to shadow someone in the workplace; if not, create the opportunity yourself. Research what fields have the most career/job opportunity and see if any spark his interest. Remember, many students begin college without declaring a major.

Challenge	Solution
Your teenager wants to major in music in college. You think a degree in music is worthless.	Now is the time to listen to your teenager's dream. Discuss a career in music and research the possibilities it offers. Contact the music department of a university and possibly arrange a visit for your son. Stay open to his ideas.
Your teenager tells you he has decided to join the armed forces. This information catches you off guard.	Again, remember that this is his decision. Be supportive and ask him what research he has done. Does he know which branch he wants to join? What is his objective with the military? Arrange for him to meet with one of your friends who spent time in the military. Ask him if he has considered college and the military. Have him research college ROTC programs and education incentives offered by the military.

Ask yourself: What do you do when your child's high school has a career day or some similar activity? How much interest do you show in your child's experiences and impressions concerning future occupational options? Have you taken her to work? Have you arranged for her to go with a friend to another workplace? And, possibly of most importance, can you listen to your child's dreams and keep your own dreams silent?

Chapter 3

Functioning on Their Own:
Is Your Teenager Able?

The question of whether or not a student is capable of succeeding in college is one that parents, together with teachers and counselors, tend to consider in narrow terms. We worry about whether or not our students' grades in middle school and high school will be high enough, and whether they will successfully meet the college requirements for admission. In reality, however, when considering a teenager's ability to be a successful college student, the criteria for success need to be expanded considerably. Academic skills that are traditionally associated with successful college experiences are indeed vitally important (see Chapter 5), but also crucial are other basic living skills that must be developed and honed while kids are in high school, or even earlier, if they are to thrive in a university environment.

Consider this issue from the viewpoint of the college or university. As institutions, colleges and universities must be able to make certain assumptions about their students in order to function efficiently. These assumptions are made in three basic areas: (1) dorm or apartment living, (2) self-management, and (3) academic preparedness. They are placed in this order because if the assumptions involved in the first two categories are not met, those of the third category are mostly irrelevant.

Dorm or apartment living

Living away from home for the first time presents challenges that many teenagers have never faced; challenges that range from coping with incompatible roommates to waking up without a parent alarm clock.

Waking up on time

The most basic skill that schools assume students can manage is the ability to get themselves up every morning and make it to class in spite of late hours most nights. Schools also assume that students can successfully negotiate through conflicts with roommates or will ask for help if needed, that students know how to maintain personal boundaries, and that students know how to watch out for their own personal safety. Of this list of basic living tasks, the one most likely to leave parents rolling their eyes is the difficulty teenagers have in waking up. Difficulty waking up can be linked to several factors, but regardless of the reason, the college student that wants to make it to class must be able to wake himself up and get moving.

Loretta has four children, all of whom experience different degrees of difficulty waking up in the morning. It is her fifteen-year-old son, however, who takes waking up to extremes. Loretta said that Manny sleeps so deeply that he never hears the alarm clock that is buzzing right beside his bed. Loretta, whose bedroom is on another floor, can hear it. Loretta always has to wake up Manny, but even if he sits up in bed and talks to her, she knows that when she turns around, he will be asleep again. The one thing that does work: she throws a glass of water in his face. The shock and the wet bed keep him from falling back to sleep.

Sometimes, household members other than Mom or Dad join the effort to oust the sleepy teen from bed.

Katherine has three children, all grown and gone from home. While in high school, her two daughters managed to get up and go, but her son always required numerous reminders that he was going to be late. Lingering at home to be sure he was awake often made Katherine late to work herself. Finally,

Katherine gave up and told her son he was on his own. He would usually make it to school on time, either by skipping breakfast or by his younger sister filling in as the snooze alarm. When Katherine's son went to college out-of-state, he decided to live with his grandmother to save money. Guess what? Grandma did the waking, always worried that he wouldn't get to class on time.

Although Katherine's son had his grandmother to fill in as alarm clock, he is a rare exception. In interviewing dorm resident assistants (RA) on this issue, the stories are consistent. Students who cannot perform the simple task of getting themselves up and out the door each morning face a critical situation from the first day of class. It is clearly not the RA's job to go around to every room on weekdays pounding on the door like a camp counselor, yet RAs inevitably find themselves worrying about some of the students they see falling further and further behind.

Robin was an RA who did take on the job of alarm clock for a particular student after consulting with the hall director. The freshman student in question had already experienced a disastrous first semester, and a few weeks into spring term she was continuing her now-established pattern—oversleep, rationalizing that she could not face going to class until she was caught up with the work, and go back to bed—with the same behavior again the next day. Fortunately for her, Robin began coming to her room first thing each morning, pressuring and encouraging her to go to class. By midterm the student had successfully become involved with her classes and was able, on her own, to complete the term in reasonably good shape.

A happy ending, but one based almost entirely on the concern of one young RA for another student. Since RAs in some schools are responsible for thirty to fifty students—and their job is not generally defined as "Parent Away from Home"—it is also a relatively rare ending.

Just how do we train our teenagers to perform the simple task of waking up? While doctors and researchers instruct parents to set bedtime routines and schedules to help teenagers get enough sleep, most parents realize that is about as easy as getting their son or daughter to mop the bathroom floor every Saturday morning. Trying to make them go to bed earlier doesn't usually work. Well-established research has shown that most teenagers function on a late night–late morning clock—one that punches out anywhere from 11 p.m. to 2 a.m. and punches in around noon. Parents can, however, let natural consequences be the wake-up incentive for teenagers. A few suggestions:

1. Let your student's school dish out the punishment. Most high schools have a tardy policy: a set number of tardies counts as an unexcused absence and, when absences or tardies add up, the school administers some type of consequence. Many schools will remove a student from class if he or she has more than a certain number of unexcused absences.
2. If distances allow, clearly inform your student that he is on his own if he misses the bus or his ride to school. Have a set of consequences ready if he decides just to skip school.
3. The perfect time to let your student realize the "real-life" consequences of being late is when she has a summer job. Do not be her alarm clock. If she is late often enough, most likely she will be fired. The message doesn't get much clearer than that.

Coping with roommates

Even if the student is able to master waking up on time, she also is expected to handle other dorm or apartment living issues. Successfully getting along with one or more roommates is a considerably more complex task, particularly since most students today have grown up without having to share a bedroom with anyone, much less with someone they barely know. Handling conflict or a stressful situation successfully is something the student needs to learn before moving into cramped dorm quarters. The

National Youth Violence Resource Center in Maryland offers suggestions for successful conflict management skills at home:

- Set the rules for disputes: no yelling, name-calling, or interrupting.
- Take turns letting each person make his or her point without interruption.
- Find the common ground on which everyone can agree, and determine priorities for each person.
- Brainstorm solutions that have at least one benefit for everyone involved.
- Compromise is inevitable. Choose the most beneficial solution.

Setting personal boundaries and playing it safe

Learning to negotiate social interactions on a scale much larger than previously experienced is a challenge for most freshmen. Echoing what has already been stated, campus police personnel who were interviewed said that setting personal boundaries and staying safe are lessons that also need to be taught early, well before our eighteen-year-old waves us good-bye some August afternoon. Parents may believe their students already know how to say no and how to be safe, but often the obvious flies over their heads:

- Lock dorm rooms; people steal. Laptops and MP3 players are hot targets; keep them within reach or locked up.
- Be careful about who has access to your room; that young woman you just met at the party might lift your cash when you slip out to get her a soda.
- Avoid being alone with someone you don't know; the young man you just met may become aggressive when you decide to leave.
- Always be aware of your surroundings; if you're left late at night to walk home alone, you may find yourself in a vulnerable situation.

As one campus officer put it, "The dilemma is, we try to make the dorms a friendly, relaxed atmosphere, but then we end up encouraging the behaviors that leave people vulnerable."

Self-management

Another assumption that colleges make regarding incoming freshmen is that a student has a high level of self-management skills. It is expected that a student can pace herself, keep herself organized enough to maintain her course work and her social life on a sustained basis (at least through a semester), can recognize when she is becoming too stressed emotionally or physically, and can ask for help if needed. While it seems logical that the habitually disorganized student who struggled to remember homework assignments in high school may face the same troubles in college, it may come as a surprise that the " superfunctional" high school student also may run into self-management problems.

Midsemester, a student came to see her instructor during office hours. As Jessica, a second semester sophomore, entered the office she was noticeably nervous. "I don't understand why I'm having such a hard time this semester," she said. "I'm getting a C in your class, and I've never gotten Cs before." Further questioning revealed that Jessica was, in fact, getting Cs in a number of her classes. In high school, she said, this had never happened.

"How many credit hours are you taking?" the instructor asked. Turned out, Jessica was taking eighteen credit hours (one class more than standard for a full-time student), was working two part-time jobs, volunteered each week in two local social service agencies, and was living in a house with eleven other people. She was majoring in psychology but spending most of her energy on her music classes. Music was her real passion, but she was firmly convinced that majoring in music would never get her a job.

After a few more minutes of conversation concerning Jessica's growing feelings of confusion and general burnout, the instructor suggested she take some time off during the summer to think about what she really wanted to do. There are careers that combine psychology and music, the instructor pointed out, but it was also possible that she was simply overextended. "It seems to me," the teacher said, "that you need to slow down long enough to look at things, to think about what you want to be doing right now."

"But I'm going to summer school," Jessica protested. "The summer term starts the Monday after final exam week. I need to graduate in three years, and that's the only way I can."

What is difficult for the faculty member or advisor in a situation such as the one just described is to determine from where the pressure is coming. In particular, how much of the pressure represents the parents' wishes? While the image of the draconian parent standing over the beleaguered student, whip in hand, may be tempting to buy into, oftentimes the truth is that the students themselves are putting on the pressure and then using their parents as a form of legitimization. "My dad will kill me," actually may only be a way of saying that the student is in over her head and needs help managing her many activities, including a reality check of what is even possible. In either case, the point is that whether your high school student was the disorganized but engaging young man whose dreams and wit seemed to carry him through anything, or the overachieving and serious scholar with an updated filing system in her backpack, at college students will be, for the most part, on their own.

Having said that, it is necessary to amend the "they're on their own" statement in a crucial way. All colleges and universities have services available to help students with an array of issues. Your student's academic advisor is only one such person, and too often students feel that the advisor assigned to them as an incoming college freshman is the only source of guidance. In reality, colleges have entire departments devoted to support services for students, whether it is traditional academic advising, emotional counseling, or assistance with issues such as test anxiety or time management. Looking for those services is not something that comes automatically to most students—students need to come to college with that skill already semipolished. The place for your student to learn to ask for and use resources is in high school. Does your teenager venture forth to the counselor's office in search of information or do you do it for her? Who checks into missing assignments when your child is absent? Is your sixteen-year-old willing to make an appointment to talk to his teacher when he just doesn't get that math problem? The more teenagers learn to seek help while in high school, the more likely they will do so at college.

From the beginning of his education, Levi's parents encouraged him to talk with his teachers when he didn't understand something, so once he hit high school, Levi would seek out his teachers during an off period, at lunch, or after school to figure out a math problem or clarify a chemistry equation. Although his mother prompted him, she gave Levi the responsibility to pick up college and scholarship information from the counselor's office. On his own, Levi made appointments to ask his counselor's advice on course selections and college issues.

Things went well for Levi during his first semester at the University of Colorado. But during midterm exams of his second semester, Levi called home at 10:00 one morning in a panic.

"Mom, I've overslept my midterm! It's getting out right about now. What am I going to do?"

His mother, feeling a little panicked herself, suggested he find the professor and try to work things out. Levi, who really knew that already, immediately called the professor's phone and left a message explaining what happened. He went to the department office and left another message. He sent an e-mail. Within an hour after missing his exam, Levi had done everything possible to contact his professor who had already left the CU campus that day. As it turned out, Levi left a couple more messages, but did not hear from the professor until the next class meeting. The professor acknowledged all of Levi's efforts and let him take a make-up exam with no penalty.

Because Levi had been trained before college to ask questions and seek help, he did not hesitate to take care of the issue immediately. Will your teenager be able to manage his time and energy effectively, and will he recognize when he needs help and then act on that realization? Furthermore, will your student, like Levi, be willing to try all avenues and look to alternative sources of help if the first attempt is a bust? This is no small task, particularly when you consider that many parents have problems asking for help themselves. And this is not even dealing with the "I can handle it" imperative that most students feel as they prepare to move beyond high school after months of anticipation. It is while they are still in high school, therefore, that parents need to demonstrate to their student that they are not above checking with counselors or teachers about how their kids are doing, not above questioning whether the student is taking on too much of a workload, and not too proud to admit a need to reorganize activities, reprioritize goals, or seek professional help on occasion.

Sherisa made straight As throughout her high school years. A motivated student, Sherisa set off for the University of California at Riverside with high academic expectations; her parents held the same expectations. It took her by surprise, therefore, when she found herself struggling in a math class her first semester. When Sherisa received a B on a math test, she became nervous and depressed, certain her academic achievements were starting a downturn. After crying in her dorm room for a couple of days, Sherisa sought the counsel of her RA. The RA suggested Sherisa visit the campus health center and make an appointment with a counselor who could help bring perspective to Sherisa's issues. In counseling, Sherisa unloaded her stress and learned relaxation techniques, became more realistic about her schoolwork and grades, and gained the confidence she needed to proceed.

Sherisa showed that she recognized when she needed to ask for help. She was able to locate and use resources to help her get through a difficult time without becoming overwhelmed and giving up on college life and its demands.

Classroom participation

As stated earlier, when most parents think about preparing their students for college academically, they tend to look first at grades and test performance numbers, then maybe some of the self-management issues outlined above. This is logical. After all, these are the areas so relevant for admission to a college or university. However, to go a bit deeper, what most faculty are assuming—and understand that they have not seen and will never see students' transcripts, SAT scores, etc.—is that new students have mastered reading, writing, and computing skills to the extent that they can keep up with class work or recognize when they need additional help; that they have enough knowledge in areas such as history and literature to follow a class discussion that includes these topics (even in math and science classes); that they can think analytically and will question both the texts and teachers when the information does not quite fit with their understanding of the material; and that they are willing and able to actively participate in class even if it may not seem the cool thing to do. Inside and outside the classroom, not asking for help has been observed and reported by counselors, parents, students, and teachers as a major stumbling block. This last item represents a common high school dynamic.

High school teachers often give points based on class participation in an effort to encourage dialogue and questions, pumping kids to think and consider beyond the requirements of the class. Logan took calculus in his last year of high school, a subject he considered a complete waste of time. His teacher, however, noted that Logan always had his hand up, asking that a problem be clarified, sometimes more than once. His teacher told his parents that he appreciated Logan's constant questions because so few kids in the class ever asked anything, and the teacher knew that most needed the clarification.

Once he got to college, Logan continued to ask questions, even when he was one in a class of three hundred students. If he needed help, Logan would seek out the teaching assistant or make an appointment to see his professor. Logan learned persistence in high school and used that skill to his advantage in his college classes.

Not all college faculty actually desire student participation in classroom discussions, but most do, and those who do will immediately note, and appreciate, the student who is not afraid to raise her hand even if what she says is not on track. First semester freshmen, like high school students, are liable at times to stare, roll their eyes, check out, or otherwise sanction those who actively participate as "sucking up." Being labeled a nerd or brownnoser just because you answer a teacher's question is a real pressure for middle and senior high school students, and how they handle that pressure will follow them to college. Unlike high school, however, participating in class discussions or dropping by the teacher's office may be, in fact, the only way in which a college faculty member will come to know the student as an individual. The following example plays out this situation.

Dr. Baker, a professor of plant breeding and genetics, says he gives four tests a semester in his plant genetics class. In an effort to get students motivated, he offers ten bonus points for any student who will come to his office and talk after failing a test. If a student follows up, Dr. Baker asks the student what he or she thinks happened, then launches into his real purpose—giving the student tips on how to study. "There are many kids who do not know how to study," he said. Dr. Baker stresses attending class, reading the text, and taking notes, then actually explains a method of condensing the notes and making them into a manageable study format.

Dr. Baker remembered one student who took full advantage of the offer. The student showed up for the ten bonus points and seriously followed Dr. Baker's study guidelines. The student made As on his next exams, made an A-plus on the final, and finished the course with an A despite failing the first test. "Long after that class was over, that particular student continued to stop by and visit with me," Dr. Baker said. Not only did that student learn important study skills by speaking to Dr. Baker, but he also developed a lasting relationship with his professor.

Assessing your teenager's academic readiness

Parents usually assume that it is, primarily, the responsibility of their student's middle school and high school teachers to prepare them academically. After all, that is what they are paid to do, right? Realistically, however, parents must acknowledge that no one institution can achieve these goals without help. Whatever your relationship with your child's school—whether you see his high school as one of the best or one of the worst—the fact remains that all schools are institutions (even the small, alternative schools), and they have your child for only a few hours each day, giving them a limited influence on his or her academic development. Grades and standardized test scores are only partial indicators of students' skills and knowledge, but those are the indicators colleges use when screening applicants for admission. The college your child attends has no other choice than to make generalized assumptions, not individualized assessments.

To prepare your child for college, therefore, you need to do your own assessments. If you see that there are gaps—that your student has not been required to learn appropriate citation formats for writing research papers, that she is convinced that correct spelling and grammar are unimportant for non-English class papers, that she does not know how to take notes during lectures, that she cannot outline information in the text—then you will need to do something about it to help her succeed in college.

You have many avenues to make your assessment—many of which you probably already use. First is back-to-school night, from which you leave laden with teacher information and outlines of the courses your child is taking. Armed with that information, follow through—ask your child what the class is working on in World History. Ask about specific projects, assignments, and tests: When are assignments due? Does your child need supplies for a special project? What did he or she make on that algebra test? If the answer is a C or D, it is a good time to ask if there are extra study periods or tutors to help. Attend parent-teacher conferences and get the update on your student's participation, grades, and deficiencies. Most schools offer an online summary of your child's grades, complete with a list of assignments and their corresponding grade, for which you most likely will need your student's ID, easily obtained from the school. And, if all else fails, contact the teacher. Most teachers appreciate a parent's concern and respond quickly. Together you can determine strategies to disseminate information and help your student.

In the past fifteen to twenty years, Theresa, a junior high and high school English teacher, has seen a definite switch in the attitude of her students. "They seem to think that if they show up for class, they should get a good grade," Theresa said of students today. In the past, she saw that attitude in only two or three kids per class, but now it seems the majority feel that way. One year, Theresa's tenth-grade English class started with twenty-eight students. By late spring, there were only fourteen. "The other half had managed to attend so little class that they were administratively dropped from the class," she said.

"A lot of parents say that their child is bored," she continued. "It's not that they are bored, it's that they're lazy." Much of the time when a student says he or she doesn't like a class it is because of the workload, she said. They just don't seem to have a good work ethic.

Learning that work ethic and the importance of doing a good job in school will eventually effect the way those students perform in the working world. In Theresa's experience, it makes a huge difference when parents are involved and communicate with teachers. Unfortunately, Theresa said, "The parents who don't need to come to parent-teacher conferences (because their child is doing so well in school) are the ones who always come, while the parents who should come are so beaten down by the time their child is in high school that they give up and don't come. Those parents are out of ideas."

As Theresa explained, when parents come to conferences or seek meetings with teachers and other school officials, they learn what resources the school has to offer. Schools often have programs designed to connect students with a particular teacher who serves as a mentor, a sounding board, or simply an adult with whom that student can connect and build a relationship.

"No doubt, parents make the difference," Theresa said. "Kids in high school may look like adults, but part of a parent's job is to guide them away from making crushing choices." She believes that some parents let kids make too many decisions that really hurt them, such as not turning in schoolwork. As those missed assignments pile up, the grades fall; it looks hopeless and the student often quits trying. Theresa said, "If you let them make destructive decisions continually, they'll never get to the point where they can succeed."

If students don't succeed in high school, it may be years before they can face the idea of higher education. It is important to discover your child's academic shortcomings, then become his advocate, even when he resists; however, do not think that you must bring him up to par yourself. Most of us have nowhere near that kind of time and either have forgotten algebraic equations and proper citation or maybe never really knew them. There are, however, a variety of options you can explore, including services available either through your school district, as Theresa pointed out, or through the community:

1. Start by discussing your concerns with your student's teacher. The teacher and/or school can offer extra help such as student tutors, or if you live in a university town, college tutors most likely are available also.
2. Some middle schools and high schools offer courses designed to teach organization, note taking, and study skills; AVID (Advancement Via Individual Determination) is one example.
3. Look to your community for businesses that tutor and teach study skills.
4. If your student needs to learn or review the basic requirements of writing a term paper, a summer English composition course at a local community college, even if the credits do not transfer, could play a major role in boosting your student's performance levels once he or she is in college.

There are also remedial programs available to students once they have entered college; this option should be considered, but taking these courses often means that graduation will take longer to achieve, and students often suffer from the awareness that they need special help to catch up. You will not know whether this is desirable or necessary unless you actively evaluate your student's high school academic skills.

The following is an example of how these principles can be applied.

At a young age, Anthony was diagnosed with severe dyslexia. Articulating his thoughts was difficult and frustrating, so as a child, Anthony displayed combative behavior in the classroom. His parents were encouraged to put him in a special school and to discourage any ideas of college. Although Anthony's parents understood his learning disability, it was a high school counselor who recognized his potential and helped Anthony pursue his goal of higher education. He received tutoring and other assistance, graduated high school, and was accepted to a small liberal arts college in Colorado. He is currently in his second year, works with the Learning Assistance Center at the college, and is doing well.

Stay involved with your teenager's academic preparedness and be his advocate. Attend parent-teacher conferences, work together with teachers, and seek help from community sources to make a realistic evaluation of your teenager's academic abilities. Armed with such knowledge, you are ready to help your teenager overcome any shortcomings.

Preparing Your Teenager: Developing Self-Management Skills

Developing your teenager's "able-ness" for the demands he will face in college is an ongoing job. Teach him conflict management, guide him to get the help he needs, and model involvement and self-advocacy.

1) Provide your teenager with opportunities to learn time management skills.

Challenge	Solution
Your teenager is impossible to wake up in the morning. You shake and threaten him, but it takes several efforts to get him out of bed.	Find out what his school's policy is on tardies, then tell him firmly that you cannot be responsible for waking him every morning. Together find the best alarm clock system that works for him, then let him work through it. Most likely there will be tardies and notices from the school, but stand your ground. This is an important skill to learn. Another reinforcement of this skill comes with a summer job. Let him be responsible for getting to work on time and face the consequences from an employer if he is continuously late.
Your teenager is on the tennis team, volunteers once a week at the library for community service credit, plays in the school jazz band, and holds a part-time job. Lately his grades have started to slip and a couple of teachers have e-mailed to say he is falling asleep in class.	Hold a meeting with your teenager to discuss time management and to list his priorities. School should be number one on the list. Ask him how much time each activity requires and guide him to see he needs to give up at least one activity (not school!) for a specific amount of time. Then revisit the issue in three months to see if things are working better for him.

Challenge	Solution
Your teenager is a good student, is on student council, is active in the school theater group, is on the cross-country team, and takes piano lessons outside of school. He tells you he feels stretched thin and wants to drop piano lessons. You think he is a talented pianist and you don't want him to give it up.	Stop and listen to his request. Ask him why he thinks piano is the right activity to give up. Ask him if he has considered giving up any other activity instead. Be willing to respect his decision and recognize that he is prioritizing and working on time management skills.

2) Guide your teenager to help herself.

Challenge	Solution
An algebra class is proving tough for your teenager. She complains about the teacher and brings home low test scores. She starts her homework but gives up quickly.	Find out if she has asked the teacher for extra help. If the answer is no, ask her to start by setting up a meeting with her teacher. Volunteer to join the meeting if she feels insecure, but let her do the talking. Ask her to find out if there are any extra study sessions, tutors, or online resources to help. Make sure she does the research and follows through, but find out yourself also. Praise her for looking for solutions and, if her grades improve, be sure to point out the benefits of asking for and getting help.

Challenge	Solution
In her history class, your teenager is assigned a partner for a big project. She does a good job on her part, but as the deadline approaches, she complains more and more that her partner hasn't even started. She is afraid she will get a low score because she has a lousy partner.	Ask her to fully explain the project and the divisions of labor. Have her show you her part of the work. If indeed she has done her part, convince her to talk to her teacher privately before the deadline. Encourage her to express her fears of "ratting" on her partner, but explain she wants a fair evaluation of her work. Whatever the outcome, praise her for taking the steps to advocate for herself.

3) Get involved and monitor your student's academic skills.

Challenge	Solution
At parent-teacher conferences, your teenager's math teacher tells you that your son did not seem to retain what he learned in geometry last year. The teacher hints that you should consider having him retake last year's math.	The teacher's suggestion might prove to be a good idea, but also consider finding extra help for your son. Ask your teenager how he thinks he is doing in math. Explain to him the teacher's concern and ask if he would consider a tutor. If his school offers tutors, encourage him to make an appointment and schedule regular help. If you live in a college town, find out if college students are available to tutor, as a college student may appeal more to your teenager. Re-evaluate his situation in a few weeks, and remember to praise him for getting help.

Challenge	Solution
Your junior in high school is an average student who doesn't push himself academically. Checking his English syllabus that you picked up at Back-to-School Night, you see that he is required to write only two papers the entire year. Checking further with the teacher, you discover the papers require little research or citation. You know that writing is your teenager's weakest subject.	You cannot force the teacher to assign more papers, but check to see if your student has papers assigned in other classes, such as history or an elective. You may feel the requirements for other papers will give him the experience and practice he needs. Discuss your concerns with his school counselor. If you strike out, again search for tutors from his school or from a local college. Enrolling in a community college course or in a course offered by a tutoring business is another option.
Your teenager makes average grades, but you believe he could do much better if he only learned how to study, take notes, and ask questions.	Start with his school counselor. Ask if the school offers any courses that will teach him these basic skills that he seems to have missed. It could be worth the battle to insist he take such a class. If not, look to outside educational services that teach teenagers these skills. These are skills he definitely will need in college.

Preparing your teenager to succeed in college most certainly involves academic readiness, but it also involves much more. During the teenage years, help your child become able to self-manage, learn to work within time constraints, recognize when she has taken on too much, as well as evaluate academic strengths and weaknesses. As your teenager faces more activity choices and heavier workloads at school, she must learn her own limitations and make choices. Figuring it out during the high school years will make the transition to college life much smoother.

Chapter 4

Academic Responsibilities:
Playing by the Rules

If you were asked to name the most important academic skills your teenager should develop before college, you would probably name making good grades and learning study skills. Those indeed are important, but how does your teenager rate on following instructions, meeting deadlines, and asking questions? When your student heads off for university, he will not have you around to ask him if he has read his class requirements for the semester nor will you be there to push and urge him to speak with his history teacher over that paper he thought deserved a better grade. In college, your student will be on his own to understand and meet university deadlines and expectations, to advocate for himself, to ask questions when he needs help, to practice acceptable classroom participation and behavior, and to create and maintain a personal schedule that will ensure success. Help him to gain those skills during the high school years.

University expectations and deadlines

Once at college, countless students slowly come to realize that the repeated directive, "pay attention and follow instructions," they heard all through high school actually is as important as the information they were required to learn. Many college students lose momentum toward their degrees as they discover requirements after deadline, fail to gain a necessary signature, or miss filling out mandatory forms.

It was the first day of registration for spring semester and Joel was as frustrated as he could be. At 11 a.m. he had gone online and attempted to register for a class he needed, a class that he was actually pretty excited about now that he'd finally decided he wanted to major in economics. He discovered, however, that the class was available only to registered economics majors, and since he had yet to formally declare his decision about his major, he was ineligible.

Things got worse when Joel went to the Economics Department to officially declare. Joel was told that he first would have to meet with an advisor, fill out some paperwork, submit those forms to the registrar's office across campus, return to the department office to finalize the process with some further paperwork, and obtain a final signature from the advisor. To top things off, he would not be able to meet with a new advisor from among the economics faculty until the last day of registration. His only choices were to risk going through late registration and hope the class would still be open, or resign himself to taking another class and make sure his major was formally declared in time for summer classes.

In addition to the areas traditionally associated with preparing for academia—developing academic skills and getting good test scores—Joel learned that academic preparedness also involves being an effective, responsible college student. Joel found out that procedures and guidelines need to be understood and followed in advance, that real deadlines exist and need to be met, and that interactions with faculty and advisors are necessary no matter how unfamiliar or uncomfortable that prospect may be.

Discussions about student responsibility often focus on academic performance and maintaining a respectable grade point average. However, as Joel's story depicted, it also is critical that students and parents understand the nature of the institutional, bureaucratic environment in which they will be operating, regardless of whether it is a private or public institution. What that means for the student and his or her family members is that there will be administrative deadlines, requirements for completing an academic major and/or degree program, and financial arrangements that will be stated formally and standardized in the university's application. Unless the parent is willing to take responsibility for all of these tasks and requirements, the student will need to stay abreast in a sea of deadlines and paperwork.

May, a college department office administrator, sees students on a daily basis as they attempt to thread their way through a myriad of degree requirements, academic major and minor requirements, requirements for student internships and practicums, class withdrawal deadlines, and registration deadlines. In addition, May keeps a bulletin board in the hall just outside the department office that announces class and meeting schedules, scholarship opportunities, and other relevant information.

"Students seem to think that any adult in the office should be able to answer any question or assist them in any way they need," May observes. "There often isn't a basic recognition of the division of labor involved—the fact that a part-time, work-study student at the front desk might not be able to answer all questions, or that some questions have to be directed to another office, such as the registrar's office."

Furthermore, May reports that "some students don't know what information they need, don't know what they need until the deadline is upon them, nor do they know how to get the information once they do become aware of a deadline situation or set of requirements—and it is all at the last minute. It is really surprising how often they miss deadlines, sometimes very important ones. Students and parents often don't read the catalog, pamphlets, or other documents, and then rely on office staff instead to explain everything verbally. The office staff just doesn't have that kind of time. Nearly all of the questions we get are answered in the catalogue. To make things worse, parents sometimes give students misinformation based on something some friend told them or something they read somewhere, and then the student gets in a mess and the parent sometimes gets defensive."

It is clear from May's frustrations that college students need to educate themselves about academic requirements well in advance of deadlines. Students that take responsibility for such requirements, and who understand the university's expectations of them, smooth the path toward a successful college experience.

Classroom behavior and expectations

The issue of students' behavior while in the classroom is a major topic of conversation among faculty and counselors. As Jill Kreutzer, a retired administrator from Colorado State University's (CSU) Department of Human Development and Family Studies, put it, "Students today have experienced a lot of age isolation while in middle school and high school, with little interaction with adults other than their parents, teachers, and coaches. They may be less well mannered than students of the past; they may be more demanding, less patient, less concerned about turning assignments in on time. College faculty and college administrators, on the other hand, are not trained in the same way as the teachers and staff at the high school level, and often don't know how to handle these differences. Primarily, they expect students to learn, and learn quickly, the new standards of behavior and responsibilities involved in transitioning to college."

Another advisor from CSU's Department of Human Development and Family Studies, Janet Fritz stated, "University professors are not going to teach in the same way that teachers in high school may have taught. There are services to help students, but the professor is often not available, nor even willing or equipped to help students in some areas."

Not surprisingly, both students and parents can become frustrated by these new expectations in college, and the result generally is that students who do not make the adjustments don't do as well as those who do adapt.

Carla and Shannon were high school best friends who chose to attend the same college. Both were bright students who had high GPAs in high school. During their first and second semesters of college, they registered for some of the same classes so they could stay together.

One pattern these two young women followed was to always sit at the back of the class. They felt they were doing well in college and they managed to attend most of their classes, most of the time. Sitting in the back, they could share comments, loan each other lip gloss, ask each other what the teacher had written on the board if they didn't understand it, and do a little socializing with the students around them.

Carla and Shannon were shocked when the instructor began making focused eye contact with them, sometimes even interrupting her lecture to wait until the two had stopped talking. The situation finally culminated one day when the instructor actually confronted them in front of the whole class. "Are you two about done?" she asked.

"We were just sharing some gum!" Shannon replied indignantly. The instructor pointed out that considerably more than that had been occurring, and asked the two to wait after class so she could speak with them. As the instructor recounted the story later, the students' major argument had been that never, in all their high school experience, had any teacher called them on this type of behavior. Shannon started coming to class less often, spent less time studying for tests in the class, and turned in a research paper that failed to follow the instructor's guidelines. She received a C for the class, her first grade below a B. The instructor, relating this story to a colleague at the end of the semester, discovered that the colleague had, in fact, ordered three students to drop his class as the result of similar behavior that the students refused to correct.

This issue of making adjustments to new classroom expectations also can involve the parents, as Mary, the office manager for a college political science department, relates. According to Mary, she and her staff receive two basic types of phone calls from parents: "They are either calling to ask about various administrative requirements, or they call because they believe that a teacher has treated their student unfairly." Quite often, Mary pointed out, the parents are attempting to intervene for the student, but don't have the information they need to do so effectively.

Situations such as these become even more complicated when parents realize that under privacy laws, neither faculty nor staff can legally reveal information directly to parents other than the fact that the student is enrolled in a class. If the student or a parent wishes to file a formal complaint, he or she may do so, following college procedures. This is generally a multistep, tedious process. An easier process would be to make sure your children are following proper classroom etiquette and that they can appropriately take care of their own teacher conflicts while still in high school.

Ann, mother of two daughters in college, knew from experience that students often feel more comfortable remaining more or less anonymous while in class. She herself had spent much of her early semesters in college sitting near the back of the room or over to the side, not asking questions or making comments in class discussions, and if she was not sure about an assignment, she asked another student. Over time, she felt more and more isolated, disconnected from school in general, and began to focus on her social life and her part-time job. Eventually she dropped out of school, and it was several years before she completed her degree.

When her daughters were in high school, she and her husband taught both of them the importance of asserting themselves in class, asking questions when they needed to, and participating in class discussion. Whenever Erin or Jessica was not clear on class project expectations, she was told to call the teacher or check with the teacher the next day, not wait until the night before the project was due to call a friend who might or might not know the answer. Ann and her husband tried to model these behaviors by being involved in school activities, meeting with teachers, and asking questions.

This teaching of assertiveness, however, was always balanced with discussions about how to use that assertiveness responsibly. When Ann's daughters complained of teachers being unfair or too demanding, the girls were questioned on the details. Unless there was a clear indication that the teacher was actually at fault, the girls were told to either talk with the teacher about their concerns or focus on completing the assignments as required and move on. Both daughters are now doing well in college.

Ann's ideas are good ones. High school students need to practice sitting close to the front (if they have the choice), making eye contact with the teacher, and asking questions. They need to focus on being a student and have parents at home who seriously support that role. There is a real danger that when students go to college, they become so distracted by the social aspects of their new situation that school becomes secondary.

Self-advocacy

Once in college, if a student needs an instructor's help, that student must be ready and willing to venture to his instructor's office, no matter how unwelcoming the situation or the teacher, and no matter how inconvenient the instructor's office hours might be. Students also need to be willing to listen to the instructor's assessment of their situation, rather than assuming, as some students do, that a visit to the professor's office is solely for the purpose of venting one's frustrations.

Nick, a student at Colorado State University, was emphatic that assertiveness is important to a successful college experience. He often finds himself advising other, newer students to seek out their professors either after class or during office hours and try to form a relationship with them. "It helps," he said, "for the professor to actually know your name among a class of three hundred. You are more than just the kid in the blue hat. It also helps to have someone to ask for letters of recommendation later on."

For some students, self-assertiveness is a daunting idea. Professors can sometimes seem intimidating, and as mentioned earlier, they often do not teach in the same way that high school teachers do. Again, previous experiences with adults other than parents can help students gain the confidence they need to talk with authoritative adults. A few places to gain such experience during the high school years are summer jobs, internships, youth organizations such as Boy Scouts or Girl Scouts, community volunteer organizations, and religious-affiliated groups.

Also, parents and students need to understand that professors have office hours and may not be available at other times. Some professors will communicate by e-mail, and making assignments available online is becoming increasingly popular, but as Nick pointed out, these paths of communication do not help the professor learn just who the student is. Another factor to consider is that when school is completed, students will be entering the job market. Not only will office visits with the professor enable the student seeking recommendation letters, as Nick suggested, but it also helps the student develop the social skills necessary to make her way in the world beyond school.

About a third of the way through the semester, Hiroshi dropped by the office of his plant genetics professor. One of ninety-five in the class, Hiroshi introduced himself and told his professor that he was really enjoying the class and wanted to learn more about the field of plant breeding. Hiroshi often spoke with his genetics professor after that initial meeting, and as his undergraduate studies in biology were winding down, the professor asked Hiroshi if he would be interested in a master's program internship in plant breeding and genetics. Hiroshi eagerly jumped at the opportunity, earned his master's degree, and is about to finish his Ph.D. in plant genetics at North Carolina State University. Hiroshi's professor, who has similarly rewarded other students who sought him out, strongly urges students to talk to their professors. "They [professors] can help you with your career," he said. "But you [the student] have to make the move to say hello."

As Hiroshi's professor pointed out, a student's effort to develop a relationship with teachers can certainly open career doors. Along the way, however, students must advocate for themselves. Prospective employers rarely, if ever, look at a student's grades, but they do observe how that student promotes himself or herself. Once a student has the degree, it may well be the student's ability to express her goals, ideas, and motivation successfully to another adult that lands her the job.

Abe, an outspoken young man, had always maintained a high GPA, and he often challenged teachers when he felt he had been graded unfairly. He participated in several special programs for advanced students, a fact of which he made certain his teachers were aware.

Over time, however, it became clear to faculty that Abe was unwilling to make all the needed changes in his work to achieve those A grades. He might change one or two sentences or references, but he would never do all that was asked of him. While Abe's strategy had worked for him in high school, in college the teachers were less willing to see his approach as healthy assertiveness when the quality of his work remained unchanged. By the time Abe was a senior, he found few faculty willing to write recommendations for him, and he felt bitter and frustrated, still arguing to all who would listen that his teachers were totally unreasonable. His faculty advisor attempted to explain that either graduate school or employment would involve even greater expectations and the ability to adapt, but the advisor was left with the impression that it would take further disappointment before Abe would possibly change his strategy, if he ever did.

It is important to note that interactions with professors are often key to a student's success, but students must realize that professors may not be willing to alter their assessment of a student's performance unless they see a clear reason to do so.

Natasha was a college freshman who had done well enough in high school with Advanced Placement classes and a course at the local community college that she entered the university with second semester status. She was shocked, then, when she received a C on her first research paper in economics. She immediately called her mother and vented her frustration. The paper, she said assuredly, was worth at least a B-plus! This left Natasha shaken, since her first few weeks in the dorm had been rocky and she was just beginning to build her confidence back.

After considerable persuading by her mother, Natasha went to see the professor and asked him to explain the problems in her paper. Twenty minutes later she emerged from his office with a much clearer impression of his expectations. Her future grades in the class improved remarkably, and she felt confident that if she needed to, she could do the same thing in other classes.

Managing personal schedules

In addition to communicating with teachers, high schoolers who have kept track of assignments, successfully managed their time and made deadlines, and learned to balance work and social activities with academic requirements, are the students most likely to succeed in college. Unlike high school, however, college professors don't seek out students who are not in class to tell them of changes in assignments and schedules. Students who relied on their high school teachers to remind them, more than a few times, of upcoming assignments and who were used to getting at least some credit if they missed a class will find things very different in college.

Leslie was certain that she was on top of things at school. She had looked over the course requirements the first week of the semester, making note of the requirements in the syllabi and the scheduled dates for papers and exams. She considered herself a strong, independent student and opted not to attend her classes except during key periods, such as the class before a major exam. During her ski weekend at Vail, she e-mailed her economics research paper to her teacher and was anticipating a difficult week of studying for the midterm once she got back to school on Monday evening. As she had noted at the first of the semester, the midterm was scheduled for the following Friday.

Unfortunately, Leslie returned to find that the teacher had been ill earlier in the semester and had canceled two classes, then distributed a revised schedule. The research paper assignment had been modified so that her e-mailed submission did not meet the newer set of requirements, and the midterm had been rescheduled for the Monday morning class session she had just missed. Since the teacher had not seen Leslie for a number of weeks, he was not sympathetic to her pleas to be allowed to take a makeup exam and rewrite her paper. She received a D for the course and her parents no longer were willing to finance her ski weekends.

In interviews with university counseling staff members who deal with the emotional and psychological needs of students, one of the notably recurring themes is the importance of students taking on the responsibilities involved in becoming an independent student. In other words, Mom and Dad are not going to be there asking whether Josh and Sarah have been keeping up with homework, know when assignments are due, and know what the project requirements are. Colorado State University counselor Cindy Swindell added, "Students often have a difficult time dealing with the fact that much of the information they are going to be responsible for is in the textbook reading requirements and will not necessarily be covered in class lectures." Swindell noted that students need to understand the level of work that will be expected. Faculty assume that students will spend two to three hours of preparation (reading text materials, reviewing class notes) for each hour they are in class. This particular point usually is a major theme in incoming student orientations, but often is discounted as "overstatement." However, a significant number of students find themselves in serious trouble during their first or second year because they have procrastinated themselves into extreme situations in which they are in serious or irreversible trouble that could result in suspension or, at the very least, loss of financial support from the college or various scholarships.

When Colin, a sophomore at Virginia Tech, was asked to name the most important ways to succeed in college, he said: "Develop good time management skills, take responsibility for getting the work done, and go to class." Colin found that the organizational skills he developed in high school were significantly helpful when he made the transition to college. It probably helped that Colin's parents often reminded him that once he got to college he would be responsible for himself—no nagging questions from them about schoolwork. Since Colin is doing well in school, clearly his adjustment has been a successful one.

A major part of this picture is the socialization or training that students receive while still in high school. If parents participate in the schooling environment by attending parent-teacher meetings, working with their student to formulate their schedules for the following year, and keeping track of grades, then they communicate to their kids the importance of education and, perhaps just as important, the value of involvement. If those parents insist that their teenagers meet with teachers when problems arise, encourage that teenager to speak with other adults in a social setting, and make that teenager responsible for making doctor and other appointments, they just might create a capable student who can successfully negotiate the college bureaucracy and life beyond high school.

Like many parents, Ella found she gained insight from what she considers parenting "mistakes" she made with her oldest child. Her oldest son, Cam, was shy, but a good student who found it hard to talk to his teachers. Although Ella encouraged him to meet with his teachers if he had a problem, he usually avoided the confrontation and let the problem slide. When it was time for an appointment with the optometrist, Ella asked Cam to call because he knew his own schedule better than she. Cam usually responded: "Mom, would you do it for me?" and usually Ella did.

Once Cam got to college, he continued to steer clear of dealing with appointments and solving problems. "He would wait until the last minute to do everything," Ella remembers. "During his freshman year, he called in a panic saying he couldn't register until he got his health insurance information into the campus health clinic. He said, 'Mom, the clinic closes in ten minutes and if I don't register today I won't get into any of the classes I need for next semester.'"

When Ella's younger son reached high school age, she took a different approach. She insisted that Drew meet with his teachers when issues arose, and although he said he was uncomfortable doing so, Ella did not give him a way out. "Each time he did it, it got easier for him," Ella said. "He learned to stand up for himself." Ella also insisted that Drew make his own doctor and related appointments, and she did not cover for him if he failed to do so.

"When it came time for Drew to apply to college, he did everything himself," Ella said. "He applied early, got letters of recommendation, applied for scholarships—all on his own." Now that Drew is in college, Ella says he effectively manages registration, appointments, and deadlines. "I pushed Drew to take care of himself," Ella muses. "Cam can do those things now, but it took him until he was twenty-four. Drew could do it at seventeen."

Preparing Your Teenager: Mastering Skills for Life Without You

Remember that when your teenager goes off to college, you will not be there to remind him to check when club soccer tryouts are or what the deadline is to sign up for football tickets. At college, he will have to ask the questions, meet deadlines without you, and follow through. Provide opportunities while your teenager is in high school to master those skills.

1) Give your teenager opportunities to learn self-advocacy skills.

Challenge	Solution
Your teenager is uncomfortable around adults she doesn't know. She avoids asking questions and says very little when asked a question.	Be sensitive to her discomfort, but begin placing her in situations where she has the opportunity to talk with adults whom you know will be patient and kind with her. Possibilities include office picnics, dinners at home with guests she doesn't know, or social gatherings of community groups to which you belong. Speak to two or three adults in advance and ask them to engage her in conversation. This will give her a chance to slowly gain confidence. Another idea is to get her involved in organizations that allow her leadership positions, such as Scouts or 4-H.
Whenever your teenager has a run-in with a teacher, she complains and calls the teacher unfair. Her attitude gets worse the older she gets.	Ask her to fully explain her complaints against the teacher. Evaluate each complaint with her and help her to determine which are legitimate and which are not. Then insist she make an appointment with one teacher with whom she has a legitimate concern. If she refuses, set the appointment yourself and attend with her. Let her do the talking, then discuss the results later. Regardless of the outcome, praise her for speaking up for herself and for opening communication.

Challenge	Solution
It is time for your teenager to open a savings or checking account. She asks you to come along and take care of things because she doesn't understand how accounts work.	Agree to go with her, but tell her she needs to do the talking and asking. Have her make a list of questions beforehand. At the bank, allow the conversation to remain between the bank employee and your teenager. Afterward, praise her for asking questions and educating herself.

2) Encourage acceptable classroom behavior and participation.

Challenge	Solution
Your teenager is an average student who gives no indication of being a problem to teachers. He claims everything is fine, but you wonder. You contact one or two teachers and discover that he is a quiet student who sits at the side or back or the room whenever possible and never asks questions.	If you are not already, be sure to model participation by always attending parent-teacher conferences, asking for and reading the school newsletter, and asking daily questions about his school day. Ask him what he does when he doesn't understand an assignment or does poorly on a test. Discuss his options, including asking questions in class, volunteering to answer questions, and sitting in locations that give him the best access to the teacher. Consider some type of motivation for greater participation, such as a special outing. Continue evaluating the situation, praising him for increasing participation, which probably will result in higher grades.

Challenge	Solution
You get an e-mail from one of your teenager's teachers claiming that although he makes decent grades, he is disruptive in class. He is a class clown and his jokes disturb the focus of the class. He is losing participation points for his behavior.	Relate the teacher's complaints and ask what is going on in that particular class. Be prepared for an answer that could include, "It's a boring class," "Everyone does it; the teacher just doesn't like me," or "The teacher lets things get out of control." Ask if he is having similar issues in other classes. Regardless of his answer, ask him what he gains from disrupting the class. What does anyone gain from his disruptions? What does he feel like when someone interrupts him or doesn't take him seriously? Tell him you will follow up and that if he doesn't give his teacher simple respect then he is jeopardizing gaining respect himself. Have consequences ready. Contact his other teachers to learn how he behaves in those classes.

3) Allow your teenager to be responsible.

Challenge	Solution
Concerned about your teenager's ability to keep track of things, you have been monitoring her assignments since seventh grade. You e-mail her teachers regularly to check on what is due that week and you decide what she needs to accomplish each day. Now that she is a sophomore in high school, she knows the routine and completely depends on your keeping track. She gets angry at you if she gets behind.	While it is often a good idea to monitor your teenager's assignments, it is a detriment to her if you never let her be responsible for figuring out how much time each one takes and when they are due. Even if you worry she will miss something and end up with a lower grade, you need to give over this responsibility. First, tell her that you realize you have been her organizational secretary and that you are resigning from the job. Help her to set up either a planner (often provided by the school) or a calendar on her cell phone or computer. In the beginning, ask daily if she has recorded her assignments or looked at her calendar. If not, ask her how she will find out what assignments are due. You can suggest she e-mail the teacher or possibly ask a classmate. Gradually back off to asking only once or twice a week. Expect some missed or late assignments and angry accusations on her part, but it is crucial that she learn this before college.

Challenge	Solution
Your teenager has just started high school and she is struggling with her grades. When she misses an assignment, she begs you to write an excuse to give her more time. Similarly, she has asked you to contact her teacher after she does poorly on a test to see if there is any extra credit work she can do.	If you have been writing excuses, stop now. Go over the steps above to help her become more organized, but tell her this must be her responsibility. She may need more help in the beginning, but eventually let her organize herself. Tell her she must talk to her teachers herself. Suggest she ask about extra study sessions so she doesn't get into a situation where she needs extra credit. Encourage her to communicate often with her teacher and to follow up.
Your teenager has a busy schedule: volleyball practice, yearbook staff responsibilities, choir, volunteer work. She is almost out of her contact lenses and must see the optometrist before she can order more. Twice you have made an appointment and twice you've had to reschedule due to conflicts with her many activities.	Give her the responsibility to make the appointment and keep it. The natural consequence is that she will run out of contacts if she doesn't work out her schedule. Don't give in if she protests. It is good experience for her to call, look at her own calendar, and make it happen.
Together, you and your teenager have been looking at colleges. She has selected three to which she wants to apply. The application deadline is a month away and she has yet to start. You're getting anxious and want to start the process yourself.	Choose a time to sit down with her and have her make a list of everything she needs for the application process: transcripts, recommendations, essays. Ask her how long she thinks each task will take and help her see how little time she has in relation to her ongoing activities and schoolwork. Then let her take charge. If she really wants to go, she will make the deadline herself. Do the same with financial aid deadlines.

Succeeding in college is much easier for the student who gives herself enough time to see her counselor before registration, who makes sure she has all the documents needed to register for next semester, who understands class expectations and follows through. Successful college students know how to ask questions and get the answers they need. Start training your teenager in organization and effective communication. Let your teenager schedule her own appointments and let her be accountable. Monitor your teenager's classroom behavior and model participation yourself. Successfully handling responsibilities and following classroom expectations are big steps toward a successful college experience.

Chapter 5

Readin', 'Ritin', and 'Rithmatic: What's Important about the Three Rs?

At high school graduation ceremonies, when the cameras are flashing and the applause and hoots are booming all around, most parents are basking in pride, or relief, as their son or daughter is handed a diploma. Wrapped in that diploma is the assumption that if Sarah and Josh have made it to the graduation ceremony, they indeed can read, write, and compute mathematical equations. Does that mean, however, that if they go on to college they will read their class texts; write competent, documented, original papers; and successfully figure their way through required math classes? No, it does not. Josh and Sarah probably have heard that in college they do not really need to read their boring textbooks to pass, that it is easy to pick up a pre-written paper off the Internet, and that self-paced math modules are easy enough for anyone to pass. They also may figure that because their grades were competent in high school, they obviously will do fine in college. Consider it strike one if your high school graduate heads off to college with such attitudes. A certain level of reading, writing, and mathematics are essential to everyone's college success.

Kris Binard, dean of student services at Front Range Community College in Fort Collins, Colorado, said that although many of the school's freshman students have the grades or test scores to take college-level math, after the first couple of weeks, for example, in a college algebra course, they ask to move down to the preparatory courses because they realize they do not have the skills to handle the material. "They don't realize that high school algebra is not the same as college-level algebra," Binard said. "They often are surprised that they are not ready and they can get frustrated."

In another approach, Binard said that many students co-enroll at Front Range and at nearby Colorado State University because they do not have high enough test scores in certain subjects to allow them to do four-year university work in certain subjects. They attend the community college to take preparatory classes in the deficient subject (usually math or English) —work they simply didn't get in high school, for whatever reason—while also taking classes at the university.

In a 2005 paper discussing high school students' college readiness, Kristin Conklin, program director of the Education Division of the National Governors Association Center for Best Practices, wrote that "nationally, only 32 percent of graduated high school students are qualified to attend four-year colleges. One out of three college students need remediation." Is your student that one out of three? Sadia's experience below is an illustration of this point.

> During her first semester at the University of Colorado, Sadia quickly discovered that she did not have a firm enough base in writing and math to do well in her college classes, nor did she have appropriate study skills. "I had to learn to study," Sadia said. "In high school, it was easy to get a passing grade without really studying."
>
> Sadia considers herself unprepared in math. While in high school, a math teacher advised her to take statistics her senior year instead of precalculus. She followed her teacher's advice and then was unable to pass the math placement exam for her major's math requirements. Now she is faced with backing up and taking a preparatory math class to catch up to where she should be. "I haven't taken a difficult math course since I was a junior in high school," Sadia said. Sadia also realized that she never grasped the fundamentals of writing while in high school or even earlier. "I never learned how to outline or web (an organizational, pre-writing exercise)," Sadia explained. "I never pre-wrote at all and I still don't. I haven't learned. I struggle along and think I can get my paper organized, but I always have many irrelevancies. It is hard to write a long paper that is to the point and concise with no writing organizational skills."

Helping students be college ready requires more than having them do well in high school courses. They have to develop strong skills in reading, writing, and math so that they will be ready to successfully transition into the college-level educational environment.

Reading: Dispelling the myth

Reading in college is intense. Most required reading in middle and high school is backed up with guided discussions or review of what was read. In college, the expectation is that students will read, understand, and apply what they've learned without support, discussion, or review. This is a kind of reading that many high school graduates are not accustomed to doing.

The myth: Don't worry about assigned readings; you can do just fine in college without reading texts. There are three basic reasons why college freshmen, and some upperclassmen, tenaciously hold on to this myth. The first, and oldest, is the boasting that students do among themselves, claiming that they almost never bothered to do the reading and still did just fine. Besides, they argue, the tests only cover the information given by the professor in class, and, therefore, doing the reading is unnecessary. After all, students conclude, they did not need to read that much in high school, and they still managed to make it into college. Interviews with program coordinators who work with freshman orientation programs and support services indicate that this is one of the most pervasive misconceptions freshmen carry with them onto campus, and the hardest to dispel.

Of course, much of reading avoidance is due to the fact that some students find reading text materials a chore, one they would like to avoid. It is also increasingly due to the cost of the books themselves, which is the second reason the myth has been maintained. Faculty members generally concur, agreeing with a 2006 Washington Post article about the rising cost of textbooks in which the National Association of College Stores said that nearly 60 percent of college students do not buy all course materials. Some of the remaining students borrow books from friends or other students who have already taken the course, but for faculty it often becomes clear that students attempt to complete courses without reading the book. It only takes a few detailed questions on an exam to reveal the practice. The following story shows that Carmel was a student who fell within that 60 percent who do not buy all course materials.

> Although Kara liked her first-semester roommate, Carmel, she didn't see that much of her. Carmel had a boyfriend in town and spent most of her time at his place. "I don't think Carmel was honest with herself about school," Kara observed. Carmel just didn't seem serious enough to make college work. She went to class when it was convenient and didn't buy any of her textbooks at the beginning of the semester. Kara said Carmel only bought a textbook when it seemed necessary that she open the book to pass an exam; Carmel relied on Sparknotes (free online study guides) instead. That first semester, Carmel bought textbooks for only half of her classes. "She never studied or prepared until two weeks before an exam," Kara said. "Then she would freak out and try to cram." Carmel proved to be an ineffective student.

Students on a budget, as most are, see textbooks as the most dispensable of their college costs. If the student believes she doesn't need to read the text anyway and the subject is boring to her, then it is easy for her to justify not buying an expensive book. Texts today are routinely priced at $70 and up, and many are considerably more. If your student is taking five courses, and each weighs in at $70 to $150 in books, the costs obviously add up. In addition, publishers put out new editions of most texts every eighteen months to two years as a way to dampen the demand for used textbooks, which do not bring them further profit. Faculty are limited in their ability to counter this trend, since a few months after a new edition is published, they can no longer order the previous one. Finally, a contributing factor on some campuses is that those faculty members who are themselves writing and publishing textbooks have a disincentive to assign older editions since they do not collect royalties on used textbooks.

The third, and most recent, cause of the myth that a student doesn't need to read required texts to be successful is due to the nonessential nature of reading that lies within our contemporary educational environment, one that stresses the value of a multimedia, experiential approach to learning. Since the 1970s, educators, along with specialists in a number of related fields of research and expertise, have argued that individual students process and learn through varying mediums of communication, and, therefore, schools should actively address that range of learning styles rather than relying on the outdated notion of students as passive receptacles of information. Gaining knowledge through reading and lecture is not a best practice style of teaching in most secondary schools.

The college educational system is different. It is presumed that students will gain most of their knowledge through reading complex texts and gleaning or clarifying information from lectures. The reason the multimedia trend in educational delivery in most K–12 systems has become a problem for many students is that when moving into the college-learning environment the student will be presented with information that cannot effectively be communicated through classroom activities or by watching a DVD program, or even by participating in an interactive computer-learning program. College is a time when a student must move beyond experiential learning into a realm that is largely indirect or abstract learning. History, math, social demographics, complex chemical interactions, economic formulae and projections—in college, there are few ways of acquiring these types of information other than reading about them in a book, then listening to a teacher whose job it is to explain or translate the material into a more digestible form, and, at least in upper-division classes, discuss the material in class.

If your student lacks the skills for effective college reading, there are ways to improve. One way, of course, is to enroll in a class that teaches effective reading and comprehension. A simpler way, but one that requires self-motivation, is to teach oneself through a program such as the SQR3 method. SQR3 refers to survey, question, read, recite, review. It is a simple, logical approach to effective reading, and students interested in improving their reading skills can search the Internet for SQR3 to get details in how to implement the method.

While it is undeniably true that some students can pass or even do well in some of their classes without reading all the required texts, most students will need to read the required material in order to pass. One only need look at the faces of first-semester freshmen when they are handed their midterm grades to see this dynamic at work.

Students in the Horticulture Department at Colorado State University find they must take a specific statistics class for their major. One of the professors teaching that class found that as much as two-thirds of the class consists of horticulture students who often think of themselves as "artists," as opposed to scientists, who intend to use their creativity in floral or landscape design. There is nothing creative, however, about the required statistics class, and the professor found many of the students did not want to read the book. The professor believed it was their nonscience background that made them afraid of the heavy subject. "I gave the basics in class," he said. "But I told them they had to learn some of it on their own from the book. About one-half of the class still would not read the book." The professor explained that students could get by in the class without reading the book, but the difference between those who read and those who did not was one to two letter grades.

Of those students who are failing at midterm, some will manage to recover and eke out a C; many others will not. If a student continues the trend of reading avoidance into the second semester, the student may not be enrolling for a third term. Parents need to help their students recognize that even in today's world of twenty-four-hour television, Internet, and virtual reality, reading a textbook is still a vital part of college life. Although your student may have less reading to do if she majors in math or computer science, she will still be required to read at least some course material in those areas; in addition, she generally will be required to take courses in other fields such as history, English, and the social sciences before completing her degree.

Writing skills:
It isn't just the thought that counts

College students are expected to use writing to show in-depth knowledge. To be successful writers in college, students need strong skills in documented research writing, and they must practice editing and revision. In many of today's middle schools and high schools, students graduate without ever being required to write a formal research paper, complete with footnotes or in-text citations, bibliography, and a well-organized presentation of the material. Unfortunately, the following student's dilemma is not as unlikely as it may seem.

Breanne was baffled when she looked at her grade on her research paper. Thirty points off for not citing her references? What was that about? During class, after all the papers had been handed out, the teacher went over the grading criteria. "Reporting material from your sources," the professor said, "whether direct quotes or summarizing, must be accompanied by a citation—as a footnote or in parentheses as part of the sentence—or else it is considered plagiarism."

At the end of class, Breanne questioned the teacher. "I don't understand. You mean I'm supposed to tell you who all my sources were, and show which ones I used where?" When the professor said yes, Breanne was stunned and protested: there was no way she could go back and reconstruct all that information in order to resubmit the paper for an upgrade. In high school, Breanne had never been required to cite references, and she had no idea she would be required to do so in college.

Often, high school teachers feel pressed just to cover the required material, much less assign a documented research paper. One ninth-grade history teacher said he wanted to assign research papers, but he was burdened by the need to cover each required unit in four weeks. He was certain that the kids could not look up sources, take notes in appropriate form, write a rough draft, make corrections, and turn in a final copy in four weeks. If he let the process run into the next unit, it did not give him enough time to cover the material for the new unit. He felt forced to decide between covering all the required units for the school year and assigning research papers.

Similarly, a high school Advanced Placement history teacher said she does not assign papers because there is barely enough time to get the students ready for the AP test at the end of the school year. She spends all her time covering the material for the test and coaching the students on how to pass it. Teaching research protocol is not a part of the AP test and therefore not a priority for the class.

Regardless of whether the student, his teachers in high school, or his parents think writing is an issue, in college it most definitely is important and required. In Eric's case, presented below, his lack of college-level writing skills nearly cost him a passing grade in the class.

Eric was taking a course in rural sociology that had been recommended to him by his counselor in the university athletics department. "You come from a small town," she said, "so this should be a natural for you!" The counselor was shocked when Eric's first grade in the class was a D-minus. She called the instructor to see what could be done about the situation, a matter of major concern to the athletics department because Eric was due to be a starting lineman on the football team in the coming fall. With Eric's permission, the teacher sent a copy of Eric's essay test to the counselor. Eric rarely wrote in complete sentences, his spelling was at a fourth- or fifth-grade level, and he was unable to organize his writing to answer the two or three parts of each question. It also was clear that the teacher had attempted to grade the exam on content alone, not on grammar and spelling (it was, after all, not an English class), but whatever information Eric had gathered from the readings and lecture, he was unable to express them in written form.

Eric's problem is not as unusual as one might hope. It also is not reserved for athletes only, in spite of the stereotypes to the contrary. For whatever reason, Eric not only was allowed to graduate from high school but was also admitted to college on the basis of SAT or ACT scores and his high school's graduation credentials. Regardless of those achievements, he was not prepared. He finished the course with a D, failing to qualify for continued participation on the football team, and left college.

Our immersion in a multimedia society, as noted in the reading section, for some families also has resulted in a reduced emphasis on writing skills. We leave voice messages on machines, talk on the phone instead of writing, and consider e-mail, and especially text messaging, as forms of communication in which the traditional rules of spelling and grammar have no application. Add to this the handy spell-check and grammar-check functions at our disposal and it isn't any wonder that we no longer want to bother ourselves with basic writing skills. As demonstrated in the examples above, however, students need to know how to write. In fact, they need to know how to write well, how to effectively express arguments along with supporting facts and discussion, and how to document the sources they used in doing so.

While some high school students produce written assignments that are thrown together the night before with little to no editing, college-level writing requires revision. In college, students will be writing in an academic style that requires critical thinking with ideas and supporting detail clearly expressed, and the final draft must be grammatically correct. Students need to learn, while still in middle school or high school, to use the spell-check and grammar-check functions whenever they do use word processing and then to proof the final draft themselves before turning it in to the teacher. Be warned that proofreading is the step most students skip. If a teacher is reading a paper and finds the word "defiantly" where it was supposed to be "definitely" or "their" when it is supposed to be "there," it is an immediate tip-off that the student did not spend much time proofreading the paper before submitting it. The student that forgoes proofreading will find points deducted for incorrect homonyms or words that he or she guessed were correct from the computer's suggestions.

For several years, Poudre School District in Fort Collins, Colorado, employed a group of professionals with writing backgrounds to aid teachers in grading compositions. The "graders" used district- or school-generated rubrics to evaluate a student's work and always gave the student feedback. One of the graders commented that it was obvious and quite alarming that most students relied solely on the computer to find errors, if they checked at all. One of the most common remarks this grader made to students was, "Do not rely on spell-check. Proofread your work for spelling and grammar errors." The grader's advice: "Junior high school is the place for learning this—in high school, and most definitely in college, the paper will simply be marked lower for such sloppiness."

At the college level, most teachers have zero tolerance for sloppy writing. Instead of a note courteously reminding the student to correct grammar errors, a college teacher may take more drastic measures.

One Colorado State University instructor has begun requiring his students to submit a disk along with their research papers. If he sees spelling and grammar problems, he views the file on the disk to see whether the student has even bothered to conduct a spell-check or grammar-check. If not, it results in an automatic loss of points.

Another serious problem in college writing is the temptation to plagiarize. Too many students are tempted by the increasing availability of papers for purchase from online sources. Some students, especially those who have used such sources in high school possibly to the point of plagiarizing segments of papers, firmly believe that they will be able to do the same in college, and, therefore, the motivation for honing their writing skills is low. Obviously, there are some classes in which this will possibly be an effective strategy. Besides cheating themselves of the learning experiences involved in developing and using his or her own writing skills, however, students don't realize that some teachers can, and will, use programs that detect lifted sections of papers and outright plagiarism. Many teachers in middle school and high school do this also.

Mitchell was an eighth-grade honor student who, by the end of the first quarter, quit doing his schoolwork. He was bright, talented, and creative, but he displayed that middle school, "I don't care" attitude that sinks many kids. His mother only made the situation worse by always defending his actions or lack of action. After the Christmas break, Mitchell turned in a major English essay two weeks late. His English teacher's aide first looked at the paper and knew immediately that the paper was plagiarized—the vocabulary, sentence structure, and tone of the paper were at an advanced academic level. The aide said to Mitchell, "Wow, Mitchell, this is quite some paper. You wrote all of this, right?" Without hesitation, Mitchell said, "Yeah." The aide alerted his teacher, who then checked

Mitchell's sources and found the paper, verbatim, on a Web site. His teacher also asked Mitchell if he wrote the paper, and again, Mitchell answered yes. His teacher then asked him what some of the advanced vocabulary words meant and Mitchell, being unable to define them, admitted he might have copied a sentence or two. His teacher then showed Mitchell her copy of the original essay, to which he had no comment. She reminded him that plagiarism was serious and that a second offense could result in his being ineligible for honors classes throughout high school. Mitchell's teacher called a conference with Mitchell's mother, who merely laughed it off and said it wasn't really like him. Mitchell finished the year with a D in English and did not enroll in honors classes in ninth grade.

Mitchell learned that he could get caught, but the verdict is out on whether he learned that plagiarism is wrong or even to be more discrete next time. Because the plagiarism problem is widespread, some college faculty design writing assignments for which the use of online sources is not possible. Assigned topics may be narrow or specifically defined, teachers may require the use of specified sources to the exclusion of any others, and some may require hard copies of specified pages from source books or articles to be attached to the bibliography.

Unless your teenager just happens to be blessed as a creative, spontaneous writer, and actually likes to write, you have an uphill battle in convincing her of the importance of developing good writing skills. It will be even more difficult if you dislike writing yourself, consider yourself a lousy writer, and actually question why it is important for, say, a plumber or a computer analyst to write well. The truth is that good writing skills are essential for good communication skills and no matter what career your teenager finally pursues, he or she will need to write clear, error-free, well-organized business letters, resumes, job applications, memos, accountability reports, and a whole range of other possibilities. Even if your child goes straight into the workforce after high school, if he or she cannot write an error-free cover letter for a job application, that application will most likely be shuffled to the bottom of the pile. Any writing that contains careless errors gives the impression that the writer—and potential employee—does not pay attention to detail or is unconcerned about accuracy.

Written communication skills are still essential in life beyond school, despite our multimedia world. Follow your student's progress through high school to be sure he has the skills necessary to write clear, well-documented papers in college. Reinforce editing and revision skills of both ideas and grammar. Do not allow or encourage any form of plagiarism. If your student is not getting these skills from his or her school, look for help from tutors or outside programs.

Math: Calculators are great, but the brain still needs to compute

While you are contemplating your student's reading and writing skills, don't forget to calculate 'rithmatic. All college students, regardless of their majors, must take some level of math. The more math skills they master by high school graduation will ensure more chance of success in college math classes. Encourage your student to complete as many math credits as possible in high school, encourage them to apply that math to everyday situations, and help them develop skills to work independently.

Other than writing, math seems to be the only subject that separates students into distinct groups: the "I can" group and the "I can't" group. This is apparently true at almost any level, but particularly so at the high school and college levels. By high school, students tend to be convinced about their math ability. The "I can't" students tend to pick college majors where they anticipate lower math expectations, while the "I can" group tends to go in the direction of chemistry, engineering, and other math-intense majors. Unfortunately, the majority of the "I can't" group are girls.

After teaching math to seventh, eighth, and ninth graders for several years, Mr. Rodriguez was so alarmed by the number of girls who adopted a "dumbing down" attitude about math in junior high that he decided to pursue an all-girls math class. "Coming straight out of elementary, the girls would do well in seventh-grade math," he said, but in eighth grade, when the makeup came on, the attitudes erupted, and boys were the focus, the girls proclaimed: "I can't do math."

Mr. Rodriguez's request to do an experiment with an all-girls math class was met with severe skepticism by the school district. He found funding outside the district, but the school administration insisted that the girls and their parents must choose the class themselves rather than form a class based on random selection. Mr. Rodriguez said the outcome was predictable: several parents, mostly fathers, saw a girls-only math class and signed up their unwilling daughters in an effort to keep them separated from boys. The girls in the class were resentful and the experiment proved disastrous, Mr. Rodriguez said.

In a regular math class, Mr. Rodriguez explained, girls often refuse to answer questions or ask them for fear they will appear too smart, too dumb—too something—in front of the boys. The boys usually oblige by teasing the girls who participate. In the all-girls class, Mr. Rodriguez found that the "meanest" girls in the class took on the role of the boys—they were the ones teasing and belittling the girls who tried to answer questions.

In an interesting twist, the district also required Mr. Rodriguez to hold an all-boys math class. Worried he would end up with a locker-room setting, Mr. Rodriguez was surprised when "the shyest, most studious boys signed up. It was a great class."

Chapter Five

Mr. Rodriguez said another math block that throws a kid into the "I can't" group is when a parent proclaims something similar to what one did during a parent-teacher conference. The parent said: "It took me three years to pass algebra. He [my son] is just like me." That type of parental attitude only enables students to believe they "can't do math," when in reality, Mr. Rodriguez said, "anyone can do junior high math. It's just not that hard." The problem is a lack of participation, note taking, and studying—all tasks required to "get it" and move into the "I can" camp. What parents and students need to recognize is that once in college, all majors will require some mathematical problem solving. Social science majors will be required to take statistics and research courses; physical science majors will be required to look at the ways in which mathematical formulas translate into real-world variables. While your student is in middle school or high school is the time to ask whether their math experiences are primarily focused around putting numbers into formulas and then cranking out the results, or are also dealing with the basic question of, "What do these findings mean?" College-level math will require students to be able to apply math principles to real-life problems and scenarios.

Tom, a manager in an engineering firm, is the father of three children—one each in college, high school, and junior high. While his wife always helps their children with English and social studies homework, the math questions fall to Tom, the parent who uses math regularly in his work. When the oldest child was in high school, Tom became frustrated at his son's lack of interest in "understanding the concepts" behind his math homework. To his further dismay, Tom's two younger children are following suit. Despite Tom's efforts to get them to probe the concepts, they just want to get their math homework done and out of the way. Tom believes his children will never be completely successful with math.

Despite Tom's frustration, parents shouldn't feel that it is their job to explain particular formulas or calculation techniques, which often seem to have changed, somehow, since they were in school. Rather, it might be better if parents simply include their kids in their own problem-solving situations, some of which involve math skills. Whether it is the task of making cookies from scratch (measurement and following directions), repairing the fence (measurement and tool use), or choosing the best buy at the grocery store (percentages and budgeting), such hands-on activities remain the most effective ways for children and teenagers to apply what they learn in the classroom, and provide a general understanding of mathematical relationships that will help the student pull all of the pieces together once in college.

Tom, the frustrated, math homework–assisting father mentioned above, said that he often played verbal math games with his kids on vacation drives as well as using everyday opportunities—such as the time a news story about space was playing on the kitchen radio and Tom asked one of his sons how fast he could convert the number of miles between earth and the moon to kilometers. Doubting Tom's kids are probably picking up more practical applications of math than Tom figures, but Tom sees reason to be alarmed even outside his home. While in a local farm and ranch store, Tom was considering a forty-gallon sprayer to use at home. Information with the tank revealed the number of gallons to square feet application. Tom was amazed as he spoke with the college-educated, twenty-something clerk who did not have a clue how to calculate the area Tom could spray with one tankful. Tom said: "I do that kind of thing in my head."

Keeping up with Tom might be difficult for those of us who do not use our math skills on a regular basis, but while you are thinking of those future college choices, be sure you do keep up with your student's high school math options. Many school districts do not require four years of high school math to graduate, but many students who take off a year from math often have more difficulty picking it up again in college. Also, be sure you research the college math requirements for college admission. Many times the requirement is four years of high school math, including specific courses, despite the lower high school graduation requirement. Casey discovered that unfortunate truth the hard way.

Music and English were Casey's strong subjects in high school. He was a good overall student and was in the academically stringent International Baccalaureate (IB) program. As he approached his junior year, Casey met with his counselor to try to squeeze in all the music courses he wanted to take. Looking at his course load, his counselor told Casey that because he planned on a liberal arts major in college, he could take IB math studies as a junior instead of precalculus, then skip math altogether as a senior, thereby freeing up more hours for music classes. Casey took her advice, finished high school with high grades, and was accepted at Trinity University in San Antonio, Texas.

Trinity, indeed, is a liberal arts college, but Trinity, like most universities, requires a certain level of math for all students. Although it had been a year since Casey picked up a calculator, he tested into college calculus. The course was tough, and without the foundation he should have received in high school, Casey struggled the entire semester. "If I had to do it again," Casey mused, "I would have taken math as a senior in high school."

Casey's situation wasn't lost on his younger sister, who was faced with the same option her senior year. Instead of skipping math her senior year to add an extra art class, she insisted on taking the math.

Another concern is the fact that many university and college introductory math courses have become individualized, self-paced modules. Students often are expected to view recorded presentations, generally online, with little or no opportunity for question-and-answer sessions, and subsequently work their way through a series of exams at their own pace. A passing grade on the exams completes the requirement. In some cases, a tutorial review session with a graduate student is offered but is optional. The idea is that math at the introductory levels is not theoretically oriented; it is a process of learning basic mathematical techniques and applying them. Class discussion and participation are not viewed as necessary, and individuals are allowed, therefore, to move forward as cautiously or quickly as the student prefers.

The issue raised here refers to the academic preparedness of your student. It is necessary for the parent to understand whether this type of self-paced learning situation is appropriate. If your student does not appear to have much math anxiety or confusion about the basic concepts and how they are applied, and if your student is the type of kid who can do well working on his own and without a classroom environment or direct contact with an instructor, then self-paced learning will work for him. If, on the other hand, your student does approach math with particular hesitancy or anxiety, or if your student is the type who needs to engage directly in question-and-answer dialogues as a part of his learning process, then you will need to take a closer look at his college options and ask some questions. Does your student need a classroom environment or is the self-paced module program a good fit? Which schools provide which type of environment for students at the introductory level? And, probably the most difficult question, how important will these issues be in your student's overall college career?

Preparing Your Teenager: Evaluate Your Teenager's Academic Skills

If your student, like so many, is one that dreads writing, reading, or math, her situation could be worsened if she happened to have the math, English, history, or science high school teacher who gave grades based on narrowly defined criteria or focus—such as giving students an A on science papers that are intellectually creative but do not necessarily follow accepted citation formats or are grammatically weak—or who simply are too busy to pay attention to details such as spelling and punctuation. How can parents help alleviate this problem? It is critical to consult with high school teachers and counselors, review your student's work yourself so you are aware of the standards teachers are using, and be realistic with yourself and your student concerning any deficiencies and what you may need to do about it. For example, a summer English composition or math course at a local community college could give your student enough of a boost so that she is ready for college-level courses in the fall. You will not know, however, whether this is a desirable or necessary move for your student unless you are actively evaluating her situation (see Chapter 3 for ideas on how to evaluate your student's high school academics).

Whether it is math, reading, or writing with which your student is struggling, take hope in the knowledge that he can reach proficiency levels with help. Reread the end of Chapter 3 for ideas on how to boost your student's academic preparedness. Check with your high school and community for tutors, special programs, even help from local businesses. If your subject-deficient high school student shrugs off your efforts to help, but he truly wants to go to college, he will realize sooner or later that he is lacking in academic skills. It may not be the easiest path, but like Sadia mentioned at the beginning of this chapter, she eventually must back up, and make up, to succeed.

1) Model and discuss the importance of reading, and encourage you teenager to read.

Challenge	Solution
You occasionally read a book, but you prefer the television for entertainment. You dropped your subscription to the newspaper and you never look at magazines. You notice your teenager's reading habits are just like yours.	It is past time to model good reading habits. Whether or not you read to your teenager when she was a young child, you still need to model reading. Subscribe to the newspaper and point out articles to your teenager. Join a book club and discuss a good book with your teenager. Subscribe to a few magazines and, again, point out articles. *National Geographic* is always a winner. Attend author talks and take your teenager with you.
You rarely see your teenager read anything, including textbooks. You enjoy reading, but she doesn't seem to have inherited that enjoyment.	Ask your teenager what she is (supposed to be) reading in school. If she says, "nothing," probe further. Ask her if she has checked out something from the library lately just for pleasure reading. Try to find out what kind of reading she likes, then help her find some books in that genre. Ask her if she will try reading in place of some TV or computer time. Consider joining or creating a parent-student book club. Consider giving her a magazine subscription on a subject she enjoys. When the opportunity arises, take her to hear authors speak. Listening to audiobooks, easily downloaded on an iPod, is another way to spark her interest.

2) Evaluate your teenager's writing skills and find ways to help him improve.

Challenge	Solution
You have noticed with growing concern that your teenager has very few writing assignments. When you ask at parent-teacher conferences, you hear that teachers don't have the time or resources to grade dozens of papers and get through required material.	A good place to start is in the counselor's office. Express your concern and ask what classes are available that require writing papers. There are often English electives, such as creative writing, that offer more opportunity. Other possibilities are elective history courses that require research papers. Even a course that teaches resume and business letter writing will be useful. If the school has limited opportunities, look to the community. Research writing classes at a community college, through an educational services business, or through courses offered online.
For whatever reason, your high school junior has never written a research paper complete with reference citations. When you ask if he has ever outlined a paper, he says, "I don't know, maybe once in ninth grade."	Again, the counselor's office is a good place to start. Ask what courses require referenced research papers and outlines. If scheduling will not allow your student time to take such classes or none are available, follow the ideas above about looking to the community and online. If your teenager goes to college, he will definitely have to write research papers.

Challenge	Solution
Your teenager agonizes over writing assignments. She puts them off until the last minute, then throws something together. Comments on her papers read something like: "poor organization," "not enough detail," and "numerous mechanical errors."	If you do not feel confident enough in your own writing skills to assist, then help your teenager find resources to improve. Start by re-reading the assignment with your student—often students do not complete all the requirements. Together, ask her teacher where to find help. Does the school have a writing coach? Does it provide tutors? Is there a course offered on basic writing skills? If not, consider friends and the community. Do you have a friend in the writing or editing field who is willing to work with your teenager occasionally? Consider educational service businesses that work to improve student skills in many subjects. On her next assignment, check that your student completes the paper with enough time to have an outside source read it and comment before she turns it in.

3) Help your student move into the "I can" math group.

Challenge	Solution
Your teenager is claiming he just can't do math. He says it doesn't matter because he has no intention of entering a profession that will require him to use math.	Make an effort to model the importance of using math. Point out to him that no matter how much he wants to avoid math, he must use it in a variety of ways, such as keeping track of personal finances, figuring out best buys, and even something as simple as altering a recipe. Also remind him that he will have to take some math classes in any college program. Find out if he has asked for extra help from his teacher. Does his school offer a tutor? Are there study groups available? If his school has limited resources, look to your community. Research college or business tutors. Even an older high school student or a personal friend who uses math regularly in business could be a resource. Praise his efforts to get outside help.
Math was a difficult subject for you and you've always told your teenager you can't help her with math because you're no good at it. You aren't surprised that your teenager is barely passing math.	Consider your attitude and the message you are sending your teenager. You are basically telling her that you expect her to do as poorly in math as you did. It is time to change that message. Tell her that you believe she can succeed in math and then proceed to help her in any way you can. Follow the ideas mentioned above about seeking outside help, and be persistent. With help, she will gain confidence and she will succeed. Stay on top of it and always praise her for her steps toward math success.

Monitor your teenager's reading, writing, and math skills throughout the middle school and high school years. Model the importance of those skills in your own life and in everyday tasks. Those efforts are your best bet to showing your teenager the importance of the three Rs.

Chapter 6

Researching Colleges and Universities: Asking Questions Makes a Difference

As teenagers move through their high school years, they usually focus on the history test on Tuesday, the chemistry lab on Thursday, the school musical auditions on Wednesday, and the football game on Friday night, as well as the gossip of who broke up with whom last weekend. It is a rare teenager who thinks beyond the upcoming week, much less declares it is time to start researching colleges on a Saturday morning in the fall of sophomore year. Parents, frazzled by work, errands, parenting, and an array of other issues, also let college planning slide until they happen to read the school newsletter or hear from a friend that the in-state college fair is coming up. While busy schedules are unavoidable, if you have a high schooler or a student soon to enter high school, put college research near the top of your to-do list. The sooner you start asking questions and doing research, the more prepared your teenager will be to enter the college of his choice.

Ask the important questions while in high school

In school districts across the country there are parents of high school seniors who discover a bit late that the requirements for a high school diploma are not automatically equivalent to those for admission to college, not even to the more inclusive state schools where they assumed relatively easy admittance. Frustrated and angry, these parents rail at the school district for its failure to prepare their students adequately. Such parents, and their kids, learn the hard way that public school districts focus on meeting state high school graduation requirements rather than college entrance requirements. Sometimes, the two are not the same.

Ricardo and Lola made certain that their son's graduation from high school was as special as they could make it. Guests were invited to the house for food and celebration, balloons sporting the school colors festooned the front and back porch, cameras were working overtime, and everyone seemed happy—until the inevitable question arose: What was their son, Felipe, planning next? Ricardo and Lola seemed hesitant to talk about Felipe's plans for the fall and his college plans in general. When the subject came up, they changed the topic to something else.

Early in his senior year, Felipe and his parents chose three schools they felt offered the best programs and opportunities for Felipe's interests. However, it wasn't until the second semester of his senior year, when he began filling out applications, that Felipe discovered some major roadblocks to his plans. Despite his truly stellar grade point average (3.8), he had not completed all of the necessary courses in high school that were needed for admittance to those schools. He had opted out of any math course his senior year and had switched from Spanish to French after one year, then dropped foreign language altogether. All three of the universities he was considering required four years of math and three years of the same foreign language. In short, Felipe would need at least two semesters at the local community college to make up the required courses before he could apply to the schools of his choice, and that meant his degree would be delayed by at least that much time. Thus the small gray cloud hanging over his party.

According to On The Issues, a nonpartisan political information organization, 61 percent of high school graduates will go on to some form of additional education, whether it be advanced technical training licensure for a skilled trade, or college. The requirements for these programs vary. School district administrators, teachers, and counselors are required to address the needs of all of these groups, not just those who are college bound. However, parents should not rely on the high school resources alone.

Like it or not, if your family's educational goal is college, then it is up to you to make certain that your student has completed the necessary course work for college admittance before her high school graduation. This is in itself a daunting task, and one that requires research and early planning to discover what those requirements might be. Fortunately, most high school counselors have already done much of this research—your part involves taking the time to meet with and question the counselors and to read the materials they make available. It is most imperative, given the limited number of classes a student can take in any one semester, that this process begin with your student's first year in high school. In addition, since even the best school counselors cannot be expected to anticipate all your student's individual needs and aspirations, many parents find it helpful, or even necessary, to supplement the counselor's information with online sources. All colleges and universities have Web sites where you can find basic admission and degree program requirements. If you look at admission requirements early in your teenager's high school years, do not despair if during the senior year your student switches college preferences. Any early preparation will give your child a much better chance of meeting admission requirements.

In the above story, Felipe and his parents might have been able to avoid their situation if they had started their research earlier; that point is clear. What is less clear to many families, however, is that if parents and students have not gotten in the habit of keeping themselves informed when the student is in middle school and during the early years of high school, it may be difficult to shift into that mode later. In other words, if Mom and Dad are not keeping up with what is going on at school when Sarah and Josh are in eighth and ninth grade, and, if Sarah and Josh don't bother to keep Mom and Dad informed, things are not going to change much when these kids reach eleventh or twelfth grade.

Researching college issues can at times seem overwhelming, especially in families with more than one child, two career parents, and a multitude of conflicting schedules; however, it need not be impossible. The first step is to realize that as a student moves from elementary school to middle or junior high school, the days of the elementary school's weekly folder full of a child's schoolwork and notices about special projects and opportunities are over. The information pipeline from child to parent often starts to clog, since the student, who is now more than ever focusing on friends, music, clothing, and all the other adolescent distractions, is less likely to report much of anything unless prompted. Most schools recognize this and provide a number of ways to directly funnel information to parents, and while there may be some gaps or other weaknesses in these offerings, parents certainly need to take advantage of them.

The primary source of such information is the school newsletter—a publication full of those announcements made over the school's intercom that you never hear: sports tryouts, yearbook sales, band and choir concert schedules, play auditions, debate team meetings, and, once the student is in high school, college information. The information will vary from school to school, but most high schools provide a wealth of information for college-bound students.

Lonny's parents, Cathy and Terry, were surprised to find that his high school offered a counseling office bulletin in addition to the school's regular newsletter. The first thing Cathy noticed was that the bulletin had an entire section devoted to what sophomores, juniors, and seniors should accomplish toward their college application process by different points in the school year. As would be expected, there were only one or two points for sophomores, while there was a full page devoted to seniors. During Lonny's first year of high school, Cathy was continually surprised by two things: First, she was awed by the extensive amount of information provided in the bulletin, such as SAT and ACT testing information

110

(including tips on how to do well), mailing dates for completed college applications (letters of recommendations, personal essay, application forms, and so on), information on generally expected college entrance requirements, extensive scholarship information, recommendations on college visits, college night information and dates, plus names and office hours for visiting with counseling staff. Second, she was surprised by the number of parents in her network of friends who seemed unaware that the bulletin existed, or else had simply neglected to look it over.

For the next three years, Cathy and Terry, together with Lonny, met with the school counselors, attended visitation days and other open-house-type events at the school, reviewed the school newsletter and bulletin regularly, checked for additional information on the school Web site, and continued to touch base with their network of parents, some of whom were becoming more proactive.

At first, Lonny balked at his mother's request that he go by the counseling office and pick up the bulletin every two weeks. He let Mom and Dad be responsible for finding out what he needed to know. Eventually, however, as Cathy and Terry began turning more of the process over to him, he began to make his own decisions. "I filled out several scholarship applications because my mom was pushing me to do it," Lonny said. "But finally I told her I wasn't going to do anymore because almost all the scholarships I could apply for were needs-based, and our family made too much money to qualify. Mom finally saw I was right and quit bugging me about it. I also made the decision to apply only to in-state schools. I didn't know what I wanted to major in and I told my parents I didn't see any point in paying out-of-state tuition under that situation."

By Lonny's first semester of his senior year, he had prepared for and scheduled the required tests, had selected three colleges that interested him and that his parents also approved of, and had applied for a couple of possible scholarships. Cathy said that on the whole, things had worked out well. She was surprised, though, to see that even during Lonny's senior year, some of his friends' parents still hadn't discovered the counseling office bulletin. Some were still complaining about the poor job the school had done in preparing their child for college.

The message, as Lonny's family discovered, is to find out exactly what your son or daughter's high school counseling office provides. It is the best place to jump-start college preparation research.

Collecting information on colleges

While the high school counseling office is the best place to start your research on colleges, don't assume you will gather all the information you need in that one stop. What you should assume is that you will use several different research methods to gather all the information you and your teenager need for making decisions. Make sure that you know the majors offered, as well as the deadlines for financial aid.

Sarah, who wanted to study journalism, did not seriously start looking at colleges until her senior year in high school. Her mother, Amanda, let Sarah be the lead.

At first, Sarah told her mother she was most interested in the University of North Carolina. Amanda, however, persuaded Sarah to consider a school in California because she felt Sarah was a "West Coast" type of girl. Reluctantly, Sarah visited the University of California at Santa Barbara. To her surprise, she immediately fell in love with the school and the community, declaring that this was the place for her. She decided not to visit Chapel Hill after all and began to imagine her California future in vivid detail.

The May 1 application deadline for admission was quickly looming, so Sarah got to work. However, when she got to the part about declaring a major, she could not find journalism listed as one of the options. A call to the school revealed that they did not offer a degree in journalism, something she had not asked about when she had been at the campus.

A quick check revealed that the University of North Carolina did, in fact, offer a journalism degree, so that very night, Sarah and Amanda were on a flight to North Carolina. Although Sarah liked the school, it wasn't the California beach atmosphere she had imagined for herself. It took several days before she was able to commit to this new, redefined image of her college future.

By the time Amanda and Sarah got the application completed and sent online to UNC, it was already May 1 on the East Coast. They just barely made the deadline. Not only that, but during the process of completing the school's application forms, Amanda experienced the nagging feeling that May 1 represented another important deadline they should be concerned about, if she could just remember what it was. Suddenly, she realized that in order to receive the funding Sarah had been granted as a National Merit Award scholar, Sarah's application for the funds would have to be e-mailed before midnight. Again, they just barely made the deadline.

"I thought the school counselor took care of all of this," Amanda said of deadlines and school information. "Sarah was in his [the counselor's] office so often."

While the lessons illustrated in this story seem obvious, and as we may chuckle over this family's frantic weekend, we also need to recognize that researching colleges is not necessarily an easy task. Where do parents and students begin? How can one tell by looking at a list of colleges at the high school counselor's office which one will be the right one for a particular student? What does the "right one" truly mean in the first place?

In interviewing families, it was found that there is no single college-research method that works best. For some, the information obtained from the high school counselor and college Web site was all that was needed. For others, it was essential to talk with friends and relations to get firsthand accounts of their experiences at various schools. For still others, only a personal visit to one or more schools, coupled with background information, could bring the family to a decision with which they felt comfortable. A major issue to contend with in all cases is the fact that the student in the family often has distinctly different ideas about what he or she is looking for compared to his or her parents.

Laura started researching colleges when she was a junior in high school. She and her mom started a road trip on the East Coast and drove west, stopping at colleges recommended by family and those that she had researched in advance. "We just walked around the campuses and looked them over," Laura said. It wasn't until the summer before her senior year that she participated in organized campus visits, and by that time she had narrowed her selection. Laura also attended a college fair entitled "Colleges That Change Lives," a program based on the book by the same name by Loren Pope, because some of her college choices were highlighted at the fair.

Laura used one unusual research technique that she based on her favorite clothing store: Urban Outfitters. "I discovered that I really liked colleges that were in towns that had an Urban Outfitters store," Laura said. In fact, an Urban Outfitters store sits nearby her number one college pick: Macalester College in St. Paul, Minnesota.

While you are researching, remember that your student is about to make her first real move away from home. At the same time, she is attempting to develop the skills and the knowledge base she will need to pursue a career. Why is it then that college administrative staff, teachers, and campus police said over and over again that too few families actually visit the schools they are considering? Why are these families "picking blind" when it comes to choosing their students' college?

When asked this question, parents tended to say that they simply did not have the time, money, or opportunity to personally check out the schools in which they and their student had been interested. Fair enough, we are all busy people with resources that are limited in one way or another. However, parents also often say they could not visit a college campus during the summer before their son or daughter's junior or senior year in high school because the family had a planned vacation to the mountains or to a beach resort instead. Even though it might take some extra time or miles, parents would be wise to think about college visits in advance and plan a vacation that could include a stopover or two at potential colleges. All schools have campus tour programs, supplemented by printed materials available online that you can access in advance, so that a visit to a school you are considering need only involve two hours or so out of a vacation day. Most schools maintain staff members or student volunteers year-round who are available to conduct such tours even without previous arrangements. As much as we all enjoy the availability of Web site information and pictures, nothing compares to a personal visit when deciding whether a particular school is the right fit for a particular student—although, as Amanda and Sarah discovered, you need to ask the right questions too.

As you evaluate colleges, ask yourself: What are your student's academic interests? Does the school you are considering offer study in that area? What will the living environment be, not only during freshman year but in the following years as well? How does the school address security issues? Does the larger community and/or the school have a reputation as a party environment, and is that reputation deserved? Is the school's focus on academic achievement, the arts, athletics, or something else? What services will be available to the student? What options are available for special needs students?

High school was a time of struggle and frustration for Sam, a learning disabled and gifted and talented student. His dyslexia, sequential processing difficulties, and hindrances in speech and language made spelling and reading an agonizing chore, and math, a nightmare. Sam was, however, intrigued with concepts, loved studying history, and was a talented artist. Sam's mother, June, said that there was little support in Sam's high school for his special needs, and, consequently, Sam became depressed and angry with school. Through various programs, Sam finally graduated, one year after his peers.

June was surprised and anxious when Sam announced he wanted to go to college to study art. She and her husband supported Sam, but June knew that Sam could never tackle the SAT entrance exam. She began a rigorous search that included Web sites and the *Peterson Guide to Colleges for Students with LD or ADD*. To her surprise, June found out that many schools, and in particular, many art schools, did not require the SAT. Sam applied for the Colorado Institute of Art in Denver and was accepted.

Not only was Sam accepted, but the school also helped him with his special needs. "That was when I learned that all postsecondary schools are required to accommodate special needs in order to receive federal funding," June said. "And in college, they are much better equipped and willing to help. His teachers would call him up and say, 'I understand you have learning disabilities. What can I do to help?'" June added.

After completing a two-year degree and gaining confidence in school, Sam wanted to apply to a film school. Again, June and Sam pored over Web sites to find a school that fit Sam's needs, and again, they found the right school: Academy Arts College in San Francisco. June also pointed out that many art schools do not have "regular" campuses with dorms. Sam had to live in an apartment and make his way around the community in which he lived. "That suited Sam well," June said. Sam graduated with a degree in film, and is now "learning how the world works."

Not only did June discover what assistance colleges offer for learning and disabled students, but she was amazed at how many specialty majors were available at schools. June declared: "There is a school on the East Coast where you can major in ship building!"

Carissa was the oldest of three children who grew up sawing, hammering, and nailing in her father's custom cabinet design and build workshop. She was a talented artist who designed and built furniture that consistently won the 4-H competitions she entered. Although she had planned to major in history at an in-state college, she believes one of her high school art teachers asked the Savannah College of Art and Design to send Carissa application information.

"They sent a huge catalog," Carissa remembered. "And there it was—a major in furniture design."

Carissa applied, was accepted, and finished with a bachelor of fine arts degree. She is now employed as a designer for a cabinet company.

Although Carissa did not do much looking herself, her story illustrates the fact that many colleges and universities offer unusual degrees. Information about degrees and other college issues is vast and available, yet how are families to get all this information? Again, much of it is accessible online from the schools themselves, and nearly all have administrative staff whose job it is to answer such questions, whether over the telephone, by mail, or via e-mail. Most schools go beyond admissions assistance and offer direct parental support, such as the Office of Parent Relations at the University of Colorado. Staff in this office answer parent questions, help parents navigate through the university system, organize family weekends, and publish CU Parent, a newsletter for parents. The men and women working in such offices are often one of the first contacts families have with the school, and many parents stay connected for their student's entire stay at school. Parents may continue to call their favorite contact in the liaison office with questions partly because they feel comfortable talking with a familiar voice, but also possibly to avoid calling their student directly and thus being regarded as the interfering parent.

What may surprise parents when dealing with these parent liaison offices is that often they also are involved in sponsoring and assisting the parent association connected with the school. Yes, that's right, the parent association. While most families assume that the end of high school is the end of such groups, many colleges and universities encourage parents to become involved in, or at least aware of, a network or organization of parents who consult with the school on policy issues and also function as a support service to other parents. For families seeking information about the school, finding the parent association might result in gaining access to a view of the school that is slightly different from that of school employees.

Beyond the liaison office, individual program offices can be helpful as well. For example, the Office of Women's Programs and Studies at Colorado State University provides information on various topics including the Preview orientation process at that school, relevant health center programs on health and safety, potential opportunities in advocacy work and employment options, and various academic programs. Depending on the student's interests, whether in athletics, international studies, music programs and activities, or some other area, a few telephone calls or Web searches should yield the contact person you need.

Don't forget the old-fashioned way of looking for college information: guidebooks. There are several guide series, two of which are Peterson's and The Princeton Review. It was a Peterson guide that June, in the above story, consulted when looking for schools suitable for her son. Peterson has several guides loaded with information, including: *Peterson's Guide to 4-Year Colleges*, . . . *to Study Abroad*, . . . *to Colleges for Students with LD or ADD*, . . . *to Christian Colleges and Universities, and* . . . *to Green Jobs for a New Economy: The Career Guide to Energy Opportunities*. Similarly, The Princeton Review has *The Best 373 Colleges, Complete Book of Colleges, K&W Guide to Colleges for Students with Learning Disabilities,* and *Guide to Studying Abroad*.

Another suggestion, and the one with the most fluctuating reliability factor, is asking friends, family members, neighbors, and coworkers about their experiences and opinions on schools. Be aware of the potential risks in this approach. The positive or negative experiences of a neighbor's son or daughter should by no means be the sole basis for making a school choice. Further, if the information is a bit dated, such as a story about nephew Stephen's experiences ten years ago, there is the real possibility that things on that campus have changed. Add to this the fact that conversations about schools can be based more on assumptions or stereotypes than actual experience, and the need to be cautious is evident.

However, in collecting as much information as possible about a school, and about the community in which it is located, word-of-mouth can at times provide important insights. As some parents and students have discovered, it may be the "unofficial" image of a particular school of which one needs to be aware.

After her son Tim's first year at Fort Lewis College in Durango, Colorado, Elizabeth said that if she had to do it over she would have picked a different dorm for Tim. It was only a short time into Tim's freshman year when Elizabeth realized that Fort Lewis had two or three dorms that were considered "party central." Although Tim did not comment much on the social aspect during his first semester, Elizabeth soon discovered that Tim was in one of those party dorms.

"Tim is a very social kid and he was popular in his dorm," Elizabeth said. "He went to lots of parties. In fact, his RA smoked pot in the dorm with the other students."

Tim made straight Cs his first semester, but toward the end of that first semester, Elizabeth believes that Tim matured and got "disgusted" with what was going on. Second semester he focused on courses that interested him, and he made the effort to leave the dorm to study. Elizabeth said that if they had known before registering, Tim could have lived in a dorm that had weighted doors that swung shut automatically and thereby granted a bit more privacy and quiet. That dorm also had bigger rooms with soundproofing between the rooms and study halls on each floor.

"The kids could actually study in that dorm," Elizabeth said. "No one went to that dorm to party."

What Elizabeth learned, too late for Tim, was that, oftentimes, specific dorms have reputations. Elizabeth strongly urges parents to ask student guides during campus visits which dorms are known as "party dorms" and which are known as "study dorms."

At the end of Tim's first year, Elizabeth and her husband filed a formal complaint with the director of housing. She believed the school was much too "laissez-faire" about the student conduct code. In conversations with the housing director, Elizabeth found out that the freshman dropout rate at Fort Lewis is high. Durango is a great location for the myriad of outdoor activities, and, according to what the housing director told Elizabeth, many students choose Fort Lewis for "recreation purposes." Tim confirmed that, saying many kids simply quit going to class as soon as the skiing started up.

The preceding story is not intended to slam Fort Lewis College. Tim, like thousands of others, obtained a good education at Fort Lewis, all the while enjoying those outdoor recreational opportunities. The story, however, illustrates that there are various aspects of "checking out" a school.

Other sources of fluctuating reliability are the newspaper and magazine articles intended to give a "heads-up" on the advantages and disadvantages of attending particular schools. *U.S. News and World Report* puts out an annual list that evaluates schools on the basis of both academic and nonacademic criteria (housing, transportation, employment, cultural events), and *Newsweek* publishes a yearly review (with the subheading "How to Get into College") that includes information on everything from the processes schools use to review student applications to ideas on how to best position one's self once admitted to the university.

All of this, of course, needs to be taken with the proverbial grain of salt and used in combination with other information sources. Your neighbor's experiences may be typical or unique. The rumor that a particular dormitory is the "party dorm" one year may not be accurate—if it ever was—the next year. A survey published in a magazine where students are asked to rate their school on a number of social indicators as well as academic ones may be highly unscientific.

So, wait a minute. With all of these difficult factors involved, all of this "flux" in the system, why do the research? As the old adage, goes: "Some information is better than none." There are no guarantees when it comes to predicting the type of college experience a student and his or her family will have, but it is certain that the more one can anticipate the possibilities, the more prepared one will be for whatever comes up.

Orientation

Let's assume that your family successfully researched colleges while your student was in high school, used those skills to select the school or schools of choice, submitted applications, and have finally received the hoped-for acceptance letter. After all that, is it really necessary to attend the summer orientation program? Literally all of the university staff interviewed—those working in residence halls, campus security, advising and counseling offices, family liaison offices, and faculty members—urged incoming freshman students and one, or both, parents to attend the orientation program. It was, in fact, one of the most commonly expressed concerns when discussing student experiences.

Students who go to orientation are less likely to drop out of school. One could argue that students who attend orientation also are likely to be the most involved students to begin with, and, therefore, the orientation process is not the factor that makes the difference. On the other hand, it might provide just the information a student recalls during a crisis or dilemma that allows him or her to solve a problem and stay in school. Or it might give the foothold he or she needs to get involved with clubs and organizations on campus—involvements that decrease the likelihood of dropping out. In particular, orientation provides vital information to families with parents who have little or no college experience. These are the families making the greatest adjustments.

Another important benefit of going through orientation, and going through it together, is that it gives both student and parent a feel for the transition they are about to make, and what life will be like as school begins. The family has the chance to "orient themselves" to all of the services available, logistical concerns, and personal considerations involved. While the student is finding out whether she will have Internet connections in the dorm, which dorm cafeterias she can browse, and who will be her advisor, the parents are hearing the common reasons students do not succeed, the restrictions of privacy laws, and the statistics on just how many students drop out after their freshman year. The amount of information crammed into a couple of days of orientation can be overwhelming. The following comments were made by university staff members and parents concerning orientation:

> "We direct most of our presentation to the parents. The students are too overwhelmed thinking about their dorm situation and which classes they want," said a staff member in a career services office.

> "We direct most of our presentation to the students, because they need to begin to adjust to the idea of making their own choices," explained a counselor in a campus counseling office.

> A campus security officer noted, "While many students seem to come to orientation, only about half of them have a parent with them. Parents should look into this more—maybe stay on campus during the session. As part of the presentation, we do modules on assertive communication, how to talk to others about problems. Too often,

students either call their parents with problems expecting them to somehow fix things, or ignore the conflict or issue until the situation is extreme, and then we get called."

"We try to prepare the students for dorm life, looking at roommate issues, drug and alcohol abuse, safety, all of those areas," a liaison office director pointed out. "Most of these kids have never shared a room, much less experienced dorm life."

Another liaison officer added, "We focus on transition—both for the student and for the parent. It's primarily directed at the parents, since the students are either generally overwhelmed or are sure they won't have any problem."

"My son came back with fifteen new friends, exciting classes for the fall, and an air of longing anticipation," mused one mom after orientation. "I came back excited for him, a little teary, and with a bag brimming with information about what I needed to know as a parent of a college student."

A mom who opted not to attend orientation mused: "My daughter spent the first three days in her dorm, eating peanut butter sandwiches with the other kids. She felt timid and could barely bring herself to leave the building much less explore campus and look for services and activities. I don't know if attending orientation would have helped, but it sure might have."

Most parents, and students, find orientation extremely helpful; few, if any, feel they wasted their time.

Sally accompanied her son to a two-day orientation at the University of Colorado the summer before his freshman year. "Before lunch of the first day, my son and I attended two general information meetings together. At the meeting for his major (open option in his case), we were informed that all meetings from then on would separate parents from students," Sally explained. "Parents would not be present when the students spoke to advisors or made their schedule choices." Sally was not entirely comfortable with that.

"His father and I were paying for this," she said. "Shouldn't I at least be there to offer words of experience and wisdom?" No, was the answer from the CU counselor.

After Sally and her son separated to their respective sessions, Sally found herself with other parents participating in a role-playing exercise as a part of a session on "letting go." Parents were instructed to encourage their children to solve their own problems. Sally described the father who volunteered to act out a conversation with his daughter on the telephone. "The daughter was homesick and despondent and kept asking her dad if she could come home for a while," Sally recalled. "The father kept comforting her and asking her what was bothering her, and basically asking what he could do to help." At that point, the counselor chided the father for trying to solve his daughter's problem. The counselor told the audience that he should have said, "Gee, honey, it sounds like you are having a hard time. What are your plans to take care of the problem?" Sally made a note in her papers: the role of parent changes in college from one of advisor to one of consultant.

In other sessions at orientation, Sally heard that the school considers and assumes the student is responsible and capable, that students need to come already prepared to get themselves up for class, manage their time, consult teachers and counselors as needed, and make decisions about their future. "They said research shows that if parents have at least one conversation with their student about binge drinking, that the student tends to stay in control," Sally said. "That was a bit reassuring, because our family had discussed alcohol and drugs many times."

Sally said she also was amazed at how much parents didn't already know. In some sessions, parents were alarmed that despite the fact that they paid the tuition bills, Mom and Dad could not get information about their student because of privacy laws. One counselor pointed out that many students do not complete their degree plan in the standard four years. Sally said one irate father blurted out, "What do you mean he won't finish in four years? That's all the time and money I'm giving him."

Although Sally felt overwhelmed by the information she received at orientation, she said it made her son's freshman year easier for her and her husband. They knew what to expect, they knew what the university had to offer, and they liked being able to ask their son if he had gone to the intramural office to find out about soccer or if he had tried the vegetarian cafeteria at one of the dorms. When he came down with a sinus infection, Sally said she confidently reminded her son to go to the student health clinic where his visit would cost only $5. Best of all, as a freshman, her son did well academically and socially, and he retained information from orientation. Sally remembered one dean stating that the most common reason students fall behind academically in college is that they do not go to class regularly. When she asked her son what he considered the most important way to succeed in college, he said, without missing a beat, "Go to every class."

Which dorm?

There is one facet of the research process that can be a bit tricky—the selection of the dorm or other living arrangement for the student's first year at school. Other than the selection of the school itself, this can sometimes turn out to be one of the most important factors to consider. Unfortunately, it's not always possible to find reliable information on the dorm situation at a particular school. For one thing, schools sometimes crack down on dorms that have had a party year. Other schools offer housing programs that intentionally group students by their academic majors, and it is not easy to predict whether liberal arts majors will be more inclined to partying than engineering or business students. Add to this the factor of random chance—the tendency of a particular dorm floor or wing to develop a party dynamic simply because of that year's personality mix of students—and predicting the dorm environment may seem impossible.

However, it's worth a try to do so. Resident advisors, counselors, campus police officers, and families have all indicated that students' first-year experiences can be shaped, if not determined, by the social network they find themselves in during their first semester at school. As one RA put it, "If they are anxious or insecure about finding friends and they plug into a party network the first few weeks of the semester, it is really hard to turn that around. You can just see them spiraling down, but it's almost impossible to do anything about it." Desmond struggled with this problem.

> After his sophomore and junior years of high school, when he made good grades and qualified for nationals on the debate team, Desmond got a bad case of senioritis. He was already accepted by his first choice in schools: a small private college in Florida, complete with an academic scholarship. As a senior, though, Desmond dropped out of debate and let his grades slide. His dad, Roy, speculated that Desmond didn't have much to work for after attaining entrance to the school of his choice. Plus, Roy said, he thinks Desmond may have burned out.
>
> Desmond had learned about the college from a stepparent, had visited the campus, and was excited to move into the dorm. Roy is not sure how quickly things started spiraling down for Desmond, but spiral down they did. Roy believes Desmond was overwhelmed by being in a new place that was more than a thousand miles from home. The private school attracted students from wealthy families, kids who took off on beach holidays every

weekend—something Desmond could not afford. Although he made friends easily, Desmond felt alone and out of place.

"He was just from a different class," Roy said, "and he tried to make up for it in other ways." Those other ways included alcohol and drugs, for which he received several reprimands, and Desmond failed every class his first semester in college.

Nevertheless, Desmond petitioned to stay at the school for the spring semester and was granted probationary status. Things did not improve. Roy believes Desmond's lifestyle choices, the stress, and his anger over his failing situation, finally surfaced as a critical health issue. Shortly after spring break, Desmond was in the ICU with acute renal failure.

Slowly Desmond recovered and managed to finish the semester with a very low grade point average. He moved back home to Colorado and found a good job. "He seems to be back on his feet," Roy said. "He is a highly valued employee and the company has shown an interest in helping him get a college education.

"He doesn't talk about that year much—he wants to put it behind him," Roy said. "I guess he is like me; he just has to learn things the hard way."

Desmond did learn the hard way that the social network he tried to plug into was a bad fit for him. With the urgings from a relative experienced with the school and the lure of nearby beaches, Desmond may have missed, overlooked, or simply not had the maturity to see signs that the environment would be difficult for him. A student's success hinges not only on the immediate surroundings the student finds himself in, but also on his social skills and level of maturity, as discussed in earlier chapters. Hopefully, parents can help their student select a school and a living environment that will present healthy challenges rather than unhealthy ones.

Campus police officials and residence life staff offer suggestions about dorm selection that may prove useful. First, they advise, look at the way in which the dorm is designed. Increasingly, schools are moving to what is commonly referred to as "community" dorms, in which the intent is to create an environment that is less institutional, less segregated from the surrounding school population and community at large. These complexes generally are low-rise, rather than high-rise—two to three stories tall. They include various indoor lounge areas; outdoor patios and lawns; food court eating facilities rather than a single, large cafeteria; and often apartments designated for graduate students and/or faculty. Classrooms and faculty offices may be a part of the setting as well. Again, the idea is to avoid the segregation effect, and the potential problems associated with it, that dorms in the past often represented.

Along that line, campus police officials and residence life staff members noted a lack of community in the high-rise dorms that have been popular in the past two decades. Such officials also reported higher incidences of vandalism, false alarms, substance abuse, assault, and other such problems in high-rise dorms compared with other sectors of the student population. "A student can be a hermit or get lost in the crowd," stated one security official. "Dorms that are smaller and have shared bathrooms are often better for this reason. Tower dorms, especially with private baths and kitchenettes, tend to create a more isolating environment." Don't think, however, that high-rise dorms are always to be avoided. One University of Colorado upperclassman told an incoming freshman during a college visit that she had lived in CU's high-rise dorm known as William's Village. "I loved it," she told the freshman. "If I had to do it again, I would choose to live in William's."

One last note on dorms: Students do best in the dorms if they contact their prospective roommate ahead of time, discuss furnishings, attend orientation, and so on, so they get a more cooperative relationship started before moving in and feeling under pressure. Counselors, RAs, and other staff members pointed to roommate issues or the immediate social network as a major source of the conflicts that tend to boil over during final exam time. On many campuses, the move into dorm life requires participation in workshops on conflict resolution skills and assertive interaction skills, while in other schools these topics are presented during the more optional setting of summer orientations. In either event, the obvious concern here is to avoid the type of daily distractions that can derail even the most sincere of students in their efforts to succeed.

Preparing Your Teenager: Methods for Researching Colleges

Researching colleges can be overwhelming—that is why it is important to start early in your teenager's high school years. Start with the high school counselor's office, then move on to Web sites. Arrange college visits and ask lots of questions.

1) Research college entrance requirements early in your teenager's high school years.

Challenge	Solution
Your high school teenager is registering for her fall sophomore classes and she declares she does not want to take a foreign language. She says she wants to go to college, but she isn't sure where at this point.	Explain to her that many colleges require two or more years of a foreign language for admittance. Suggest she go to the counselor's office or check online to see what in-state colleges require (you should check too). If she thinks she might want to go out of state, she also should check one or two colleges that interest her. A discussion with her counselor is also a good idea. Usually counselors will ask students if they are on a college path and, hopefully, steer them toward courses usually required by colleges.

Challenge	Solution
Your high school junior is taking precalculus, which she hates. She says she will not take calculus as a senior as it is not required for graduation. She is planning to attend college and has already selected her three favorites.	Explain to her that graduation requirements and college admittance requirements are not always the same. Have her check the requirements from her three college favorites. If four years of math are required, have her ask her counselor if she can fulfill the math requirement with something other than calculus. High schools often offer statistics classes or math studies classes that fulfill the four-year requirement and keep the student moving forward with math skills.

2) Model gathering information, and train your teenager to use his high school resources to gather college information early.

Challenge	Solution
At the beginning of your son's freshman year, you find you have to pry school information from him. Being new to the high school scene, you wonder how to stay on top of things at his school.	Most likely the school will send you a bulletin in the mail. If you want to know when parent-teacher conferences are and when the yearbook sales deadline is, then you must read the bulletin carefully. Also, check out the school Web site; it usually contains the most detailed information, broken down by department, sport, and activity. Make your own calendar and regularly check with your teenager. Students often know about upcoming events, including the date and time, but just fail to share it with you. You might even impress your child with your knowledge of what's happening.

Challenge	Solution
Your teenager is a sophomore and you read in the school bulletin that college fair night is coming soon. You ask him if he has heard any other information about colleges, and he responds, "Yeah, sometimes, but I don't remember."	If you don't already know who your teenager's counselor is, find out now. Give him or her a call and ask how you can best receive college information provided by the school. The school may produce a counselor's office bulletin full of college information. The counselor's office itself most likely holds college resources that any student or parent may come in and use. Start having college discussions with your teenager and insist he go by the counselor's office to obtain a piece of information that you both feel would be useful. It is important to train him to use the counselor's resources so that he will be used to researching information on his own.
At the beginning of her junior year, you and your teenager attend her high school's college fair. Excitedly, she has picked a number of colleges that sound "cool" to her. She says she wants to visit them and asks when you can go. You look at the list and see the colleges are scattered all around the country.	Share your teenager's enthusiasm before you get realistic. Show her the logistical difficulty of looking in every corner of the country. Make a list of what is important to her and to you (at this stage, teenagers often don't consider the financial part). Help her narrow the list, hopefully with location in mind, then have her do further research at the counselor's office and at individual college Web sites. Plan the easy in-state visits first. Some high schools offer one or two days of excused absences to juniors or seniors for college visits. Together work out a plan for visiting out-of-state colleges that you can afford to visit and that are realistically within reach.

Challenge	Solution
Your teenager's passion is environmental and human rights activism. He participates in protests, raises monies for causes, and always strives to rally his peers. He is excited about college, hoping his voice will grow stronger in a university atmosphere. He doesn't, however, know how to pick the best school for himself.	This one needs persistent research. He should start with his counselor's office, but if his counselor doesn't know where to direct him, you will probably need to dig for answers. Start with an Internet search by subject, such as "environmental colleges" or "human rights colleges." Related departments should pop up in various universities, such as "environmental studies" or "social justice." He could then call the department and ask more detailed questions, which in turn may offer more leads. Another possibility is to ask for ideas from organizations in which your teenager is active or familiar.
ADHD and dyslexia have made school a struggle for your teenager. Despite the struggle, he is determined to go to college and fulfill his dream of becoming a physical therapist. You worry that college will be too overwhelming for him.	Push away your fear and start researching colleges that will help him succeed. A good start would be one of the college guide books for students with learning disabilities and ADHD. Call one or two of the colleges and specifically ask how they help students with disabilities. What are the resources they offer? How do they help their students stay on track? Ask if there are any former students who would be willing to talk with your teenager. Follow up with a campus visit and have your teenager ask specific questions.

Challenge	Solution
Your teenager's best friend has an older brother whom your daughter admires. The brother attends an out-of-state college that he raves about on Facebook. He texts your teenager that there is no better place to attend college. Your daughter tells you she doesn't want to go to college anywhere else. You want her to consider more than one school.	If you don't know anything about the college, look it up online and get informed. Ask your daughter to look with you and ask what draws her to the school. Whatever she names (other than the brother) most likely can be found at another college. Point out those other colleges. Arrange a campus visit, but also insist on stopping at two or three other colleges along the way. Ask her to just take a look and ask questions. If you have a relative or family friend at another college, ask if your teenager can go for a weekend visit. The more she visits and researches, the better informed her choice will be.

) Include dorm research, and don't miss orientation.

Challenge	Solution
Your family did the research. Together you selected colleges and made campus visits, and your teenager sent in his applications. He was thrilled to be accepted into his first choice. Now the school is asking which orientation session he wants to attend. He says he doesn't need to go.	Congratulations on getting this far! But tell your teenager that orientation is part of the package. It should not be optional. Explain to him that he will meet advisors in his major, select classes, and meet new freshmen before school starts. While at orientation, he can set up his bank account, find the best place to buy books, and explore the community around campus.

Challenge	Solution
Studying is not easy for your teenager. He needs a quiet place in which to concentrate. You are concerned that he will have a hard time finding a study area in any dorm.	Make sure you make campus visits to his top school choices. Campus visits always include at least a peek into a dorm room. Ask about the different dorms. Are there ones for specific majors? Are there ones for honor students? Often, community-based dorms are specific to a major, activity, or interest. Ask to see some of the other dorms. And do not be afraid to ask about dorm reputation. Which is the party dorm? Do students regularly study in their dorm room or do they usually head to the library? Such information will help you and your teenager make a more informed decision about dorm selection.
Your teenager has decided to go to the in-state college that his older brother attends. Your family has visited the campus many times, and he has even stayed in the dorm with his brother. His brother has shown him around and he feels he already knows the campus. He sees no reason why he needs to do a campus visit or attend orientation.	A campus visit may not be necessary, but you should still sit him down and make a list of all the questions he may not have answered. Does he know his major? Would he like to visit the department of his major? Does he know where the health facility is or what it offers? Does he know where the intramural office is? Even if he skips the campus visit, you should insist on the orientation. While his brother may have filled him in on the social scene, he probably did not fill him in on the bureaucratic necessities to successfully navigate college life. He, and you, will definitely gain needed information at orientation.

The time and effort you and your teenager put into researching colleges will pay off when your student starts applying to college. If you and your teenager have done the research, she most likely will have the necessary requirements for admission to her favorite schools, already be familiar with the campus, have her top dorm choices ready to submit, and confidently await her arrival to campus in the fall.

Chapter 7

Drugs, Sex, Assault, and Robbery: Playing It Safe

When asked what the biggest concern is for their college students, most parents would suggest something to do with academics. After all, students go to college to study and work toward a degree. But, of course, college life offers much more than classes, including extracurricular activities that can and do go awry. College life has its share of challenges and is notorious for providing newly independent young people a variety of opportunities to drink or drug, and be merry with their friends. Many students do not have the skill, the confidence, or the resolve to handle such "opportunities" that get out of hand. If your student does get into trouble, remember that there is no guarantee that you will know about it—once teenagers reach age eighteen, they are legal adults and protected by privacy laws, even from their parents.

It is tough to prepare your teenager to play it safe. Teenagers are experimenters by nature and seem to make some incredibly foolish decisions. But no matter how difficult, parents should make special efforts to teach their teenagers how to resolve conflict, to stay safe, to know their limits, and to get help when a situation is out of control.

A balanced perspective

As you assess the qualities of a college, your research should include a look at safety issues. College crime statistics are available online, and the colleges themselves offer information about safety at orientation, train dorm resident assistants (RAs) in safety, and offer hotlines to students. Weigh these and other resources against stories you hear to gain a balanced perspective of safety on the college campuses your family is considering.

Families from around the neighborhood were gathered for the annual backyard barbecue. Karen, the mother of a freshman son soon to head off for college, was describing the facilities she'd seen pictured on the university Web site and the programs available for students. "It is such a beautiful campus," she said. "The residence halls are all state-of-the-art. Jeremy will have online access the minute he moves into his room, and there are computer terminals all over the campus that he can use. They have so many other amenities, like the new workout gym and pool and an outdoor theater. And, the natural science programs are just excellent. We are so excited for him."

"Aren't you worried about problems in the dorms?" another mother asked. "You know, with drinking and drugs and all that? I've been hearing some amazing stories from my daughter's friends. Two of them have older sisters at school and they have some pretty hair-raising stories to tell. It sounds scary to me, if you want to know the truth."

Karen rolled her eyes slightly and smiled. "Oh no, not really. After all, you and I went to school, didn't we? We had all those things—booze and sex and drugs. We survived it, didn't we? And besides, kids these days pretty much know how to handle themselves by the time they finish high school. Jeremy will be okay, really, and he knows he can always call me or his dad if he needs to."

Many parents have made similar observations as Karen's when looking forward to the months after a student leaves high school. The general thinking is something like, "We sometimes partied when we were young and, sure, we sometimes overdid it, but it was mostly harmless in the long run. It's a necessary part of growing up." For most of us, those comments sound pretty reasonable.

There are other parents, however, who take a different view, shaking their heads in worry after hearing some of the stories Karen's friend referred to above. What's the truth? Just how dangerous is it for a student ɔ leave home and live on campus or in an apartment? Are the risks xaggerated because of media messages and popular stereotypes, or are ɔarents like Karen minimizing the dangers? And what can parents do to ɔrepare their students in advance for the temptations they will face? The ɑnswers to these questions, of course, are not easy to determine. Campus ɛnvironments vary, as do the personal and social skills of students and ɦeir level of maturity. It's also a matter of perception, since families have ɗifferent ideas about what constitutes acceptable, "necessary" risk as ɔpposed to serious danger.

There are a couple of recurring themes on which to focus. First, there ɛ the importance of researching colleges and universities in advance and, ɴ general, of familiarizing one's self with today's school environments. ɛecond, students need to be prepared so that their college experience is ɦallenging and exciting, yet not marred or diminished by personal trauma. Ｍuch as parents might wish it to be otherwise, while at school, a student's ɑfety and well-being will be largely her own responsibility.

Perhaps these themes—researching the school environment and ɔreparing the student in advance—become even more important when ɗiscussing safety than they were in earlier chapters. None of the academic ɴd social adjustment issues addressed in previous chapters can be ɔnsidered as serious or as emotionally charged as the issue of personal ɦealth and safety. In addition to the obvious fact that all parents want their ɪids to be safe, it is also quite clear that a basic level of security and stability ɛ required for students to function successfully.

With this in mind, first consider some accounts that may well represent ɦe concerns of Karen's friend—the type of stories we all dread hearing. ｈe following excerpts are personal accounts from interviews with student ʀAs, upperclassmen who live in the residence halls and are responsible for ɴonitoring the students on their respective floors.

> "It was late at night and this guy was totally out of control, and some of the students from down the hall came and got me and said I needed to do something about it," said Rhonda, a young woman in her junior year. "So I went to his room to see

what was going on, while all of them went back to their rooms or went out. He was a really big guy and he was totally out of it. He was drunk, and maybe on something else. I don't know for sure. Anyway, I was trying to talk to him and calm him down, and all of a sudden he just passed out and fell right on top of me, on the floor. I was actually pinned under him and nobody heard anything, so nobody came to help. I mean I was pinned under him for five hours! I thought I'd never get out of there." Rhonda continued, "Then there was the time some kids came to get me because some guy was out in the walkway—where all the glass wall panels are—swinging away with a golf club. He was loaded and something had gotten him really pissed off, and he was going around smashing at the glass. For that one I called the campus police. There was no way I could handle that situation on my own."

"It can get really crazy, especially at the beginning of fall semester," explained Jackie, a graduating senior. "I mean, we had these three girls who were competing to see who could have sex with two guys in the other wing, and this was just the first couple of days after they'd moved in. Then they came knocking at my door and asking me if I could get them morning-after pills!"

Steve, another graduating senior, offered: "Some of these kids don't seem to know much at all about the risks, like the sexually transmitted diseases, possible drug overdoses, alcohol poisoning. It's really amazing sometimes."

"The drug thing is worse than people realize, I think," said Yvonne, a junior. Her stories were particularly disturbing. "In our hall, there was always somebody who had drugs, somebody whose roommate was shooting up heroin, dealing pot, people passing around Ritalin. The stuff is available 24/7. And nobody wants to be a snitch, so nobody would say anything to us or the hall director even if they were really upset about it."

"Some of the RAs say we should be calling the cops more, since that is what would happen if a person isn't a student or isn't living on campus," mused Carmen, a junior RA. "I don't know, though, because the residence hall is such an unreal environment. Students need a second or third chance to straighten things out. They're just not ready for such an intense environment."

As worrisome as such stories are to many parents, and possibly to their sons or daughters, they do not represent the whole picture of campus life any more than do the rosy images provided on university Web sites. The trick, of course, is to put together a balanced, realistic view of the possibilities and then, before students leave for campus, provide them with the coping skills they will need in order to navigate successfully. What then is the balanced view and just how does a family research safety issues for a college, or a number of colleges, effectively? Just how do you prepare your teenager to stay safe beyond high school?

Researching the schools:
A look at crime statistics

One approach to answering these questions is to look at statistics—both at the national level and at those of an individual college or university. For national figures on subjects such as rates of property crime, assaults, or drug- and alcohol-related incidents, families can turn to Web site information provided by the FBI Uniform Crime Report, which allows you to scan crimes by year for regions, states, cities, or universities and colleges. Specifically, colleges and universities must "publish an annual report disclosing campus security policies and three years' worth of selected crime statistics" as mandated in the Jeanne Clery Disclosure of Campus Security Policy and Campus Crime Statistics Act. The Clery Act was introduced to Congress and passed after nineteen-year-old Lehigh University freshman Jeanne Ann Clery was raped and murdered in her dorm room in April 1986. The Clery Act is tied to federal student financial aid programs, therefore requiring most postsecondary schools in the United States to comply. Colleges and universities report their statistics to the U.S. Department of Education and make them available to their students and faculty, and the public in general, on their Web sites and by request. Such crime information and statistics often are included in school orientation programs.

"The eye of the beholder," however, is a crucial factor here. If, for example, one considers the Bureau of Justice Statistics' national numbers for sexual assault—one in five college-age women and one in twenty-five college-age men—there is the possibility that, as did Karen, you might want to focus on the four in five women and twenty-four in twenty-five men who were not assaulted. Conversely, the National Institute of Alcohol Abuse and Alcoholism reported in 2005 that among college students aged eighteen to twenty-four, drinking contributed to an estimated 1,700 deaths, 599,000 injuries, and 97,000 sexual assaults or date rapes. Does this automatically have to mean, as it might to Karen's worried friend, that a large number of college students will be injured or threatened by a golf club–wielding drunk on Saturday night?

Further complicating the situation is the fact that the reported numbers may be biased or misleading, due, in part, to the political environment that inevitably exists at any school. A fear on the part of administrators that a higher sexual assault rate may drive away prospective students may lead, directly or indirectly, to lowering report rates even when the actual rate of incidents has remained unchanged. As one director of a university's women's studies program put it, "You can't always assume that because the numbers are low, it is a safe campus. Often, the schools with higher numbers of reported incidents are those that have been working with offices like ours to create an atmosphere that encourages victims to report, and also encourages administrative staff to be open about it."

A similar concern about underreporting was expressed in other interviews with campus police personnel and residence life staff members. While the figures can look promising, such as a significant drop in reported sexual assaults over a two- or three-year period, there are often competing explanations one has to consider. According to a 2001 report by Women's enews, "official university annual crime reports generally indicate that a mere handful of rapes occur on any given campus. Universities are not required by law to include stalking incidents in their official crime statistics, or to record incidents of sexual assault that are revealed to counselors at rape crisis and women's centers." In a 2003 Women's enews report, Gallaudet University professor Diane Clark said, "Part of the problem is simply underreporting. Victims are confused about what constitutes rapes and universities often fail to inform them on the issue." In her lengthy 2008 report for *City Journal*, Heather MacDonald, however, makes a strong case that campus rape statistics are actually played up by college campuses in an effort to show they are making progress against such assaults.

It may seem contradictory that parents are advised to "get the facts" by looking up various statistical measures of risk factors at the same time they are warned that those same statistical figures are subject to interpretation and may not be accurate. Why bother? As stated in Chapter 6, no one source of information is going to be sufficient. Parents and students should review multiple sources in order to put together a reasonably accurate picture of the situation. A key question parents can ask themselves, however, is, "How seriously does the school view safety and security? What types of programs do they have in place to reduce risks?"

Schools do make efforts to create as safe a campus as possible. These efforts involve both prevention programs, such as staff training, public information efforts, and surveillance, as well as enforcement programs that include school disciplinary policies and campus policing procedures. The larger community culture within which each school is located is also important to consider when researching safety issues, since it is the rare student who never strays off campus. It may be important to gain an understanding of how the community at large perceives the student population, to know whether "risky" behaviors are treated harshly or are widely tolerated, and to note any related local laws and/or ordinances.

Intervention and prevention

On school campuses, overall security is the responsibility of campus police whose job it is to enforce school regulations and relevant city, county, state, and federal laws. These officers regularly patrol campus buildings, parking lots, and walkways, and respond to emergency calls and reported incidents. In most cases they are authorized to issue tickets, which may carry mandatory fines, and they may either arrest individuals when the situation warrants or call in local community authorities to do so. Since regulations vary somewhat from school to school, and since state and local laws and ordinances vary as well, it is important for the student to be informed, in advance, of the rules of behavior—for example, of noise levels—and the possible consequences for violations. At many schools, such policies may apply to possible intervention strategies in cases where students are engaged in personally risky behavior as well as the enforcement of more commonly perceived disciplinary norms, such as policies concerning property damage or underage possession and drinking of alcohol.

As the end of the class period was approaching, Dr. Wilson noticed that a young woman sitting near the back of the classroom with her head down on her desk had not moved for some time. Normally, he would have said something about it, to point out that such behavior was unacceptable in his class, but it was the Friday morning before the midsemester spring break and he was feeling inclined to be lenient. Once the other students put their belongings together and made ready to leave, he assumed she would realize that she had dozed off and would pull herself together. However, as students filed out, he realized that the woman was still not moving.

"I guess you'll need to wake her up," he said to the student sitting immediately in front of her. "She's really sound asleep."

"I think she's been indulging," the student replied, while waving his hand in front of her face. "She was with some guy before class, and he kind of pushed her in here and then took off."

Both Dr. Wilson and the students surrounding the young woman's desk tried to waken her, but the teacher quickly became aware that emergency help was needed. Leaving two students to watch over her, he ran to the departmental office and asked the office manager to call for help.

By the time Dr. Wilson had returned to the classroom, he found that one of the other students had succeeded in waking up the young woman, who was now sitting in a chair out in the hall. She smelled heavily of alcohol, and the front of her blouse was stained. When the campus police and medical personnel arrived, they assessed the situation and, following mandatory school policy, took the student to the health services center.

Dr. Wilson's next contact with the young woman involved a request from a counselor at the Disabled Student Services Center. Therapeutic counseling had been initiated as a result of the emergency call, and the student had admitted that she was struggling with a learning disability but had been too embarrassed about it to ask for help. Her drinking had been a part of her attempted coping effort. The center was now asking Dr. Wilson to work with them in developing a strategy that would allow the student to complete her course work. She later enrolled in another of Dr. Wilson's classes, successfully met all degree requirements, improved her grade point average, and was able to graduate with her friends.

At the particular school where this situation occurred, a strict policy mandated that incapacitated students found on campus be admitted for medical care rather than being sent home "to sleep it off." Increasingly, schools are adopting such policies in the effort to create a safer, more supportive situation for their students. Keep in mind, however, that school administrators and policing staff are walking a narrow and difficult path between providing a secure environment and maintaining a healthy respect for the expectations of freedom and independence that students tend to carry with them as they leave their high school days behind.

George Slack, training and crime prevention officer at the University of Northern Colorado, described the dilemma: "We want the residence halls to have a comfortable, friendly atmosphere. We want the students to feel they can relax, make new friends, and feel they are part of a community. On the other hand, that can mean they fail to do what they need to be doing from a security standpoint.

"For example," Slack continued, "they often leave their valuables, like laptops or cameras, out in plain view on the seat of their car. Especially at the beginning of the fall semester, we get all kinds of calls for break-ins and burglaries. The same thing goes for the residence halls. Students leave their doors unlocked and then their laptops or backpacks go missing. They just get too casual about it. For example, we had a case recently where three guys were sitting in one of the lounge areas, just hanging out and talking, and they actually saw another guy they didn't know going into and out of one of their rooms. They just went on talking for a while, assuming it was a student from down the hall looking for someone, then later discovered he'd stolen a CD collection."

Officer Slack said that campus police may be called into the residence halls for instances such as the ones he described, or for any other type of incident that involves safety issues or violations of the law. These calls may come directly from the students involved, from an RA, or from the hall director for the building. Generally, RAs are the most frequently cited link between students living on campus and the campus or community police. Echoing through many conversations with school staff members, including those in personal counseling positions, policing, and residence hall administration, was a general consensus: the move into close living quarters together with taking on new personal responsibilities is one of the most difficult adjustments students are required to make. Add the logistics of living away from home, the pressures to perform academically, and the social pressures of young adulthood, and, at times, the situation indeed becomes "intense," as Carmen, the RA, described earlier in this chapter. As one counselor put it, "It's really a pretty bizarre living situation, when you think about it." For most students the process of adapting to the situation may be limited to minor issues such as conflicts over space or music, but for some the problems can become much more serious. Police report higher call rates during the beginning of the school year and during final exam periods—calls involving theft, property damage, and conflicts between roommates or friends that escalate into fighting, as well as an increase in incidents related to drug or alcohol use. "For some, the problems seem to come from a feeling they have of being disconnected," said Captain Bob Chaffee of the Colorado State University police. "It's as if they are on vacation and the rules don't really apply to them. If they take the attitude that it isn't their property so it won't matter, if they damage things, then they can find themselves in serious trouble." They can, in fact, find themselves in serious trouble over many issues.

Sal, Dillon, and Wayne were in their dorm room after a night out that had included some drinking. Three more students, Alex, Ben, and Jairo, joined them, and the good time continued. Despite the smoking ban in dorm rooms, the boys stoked up a hookah pipe to smoke flavored tobacco. Soon there was a knock at the door, and the RA announced himself. "Everyone panicked," Wayne remembered. "Sal, Jairo, and Dillon jumped in the closet, and Alex and Ben ducked behind Sal's desk that was out of sight of the door. We hid the hookah and the couple of beers we had, and I finally opened the door."

Wayne told the RA that the noise he heard was the television, not other people, but the RA persisted and said he also smelled smoke and worried that there could be a fire. Wayne would not let the RA into the room, and eventually the RA called the campus police.

When the police arrived, Wayne attempted to keep them from entering the room, insisting that they could see everything from the door. Wayne said the police were "intimidating," but he continued to hold his ground even as they wrote him up for minor in possession (MIP) of alcohol. Suddenly, there was a loud noise from the closet and Wayne knew it was over. He drew out Alex and Ben from behind the desk and into the hall, shutting the door behind him. While the police issued MIPs for Alex and Ben, Dillon jumped out of the closet and locked the door from the inside. Wayne was angry that Dillon would reveal himself and try to lock out the police, and he tried to get Dillon to open the door, but was unsuccessful. It took much prodding by the RA and police before Dillon opened the door. Jairo had jumped out the window, but Dillon and Sal were cited.

Later that night, when the young men were discussing the incident, frustration and anger flared. According to Wayne, Dillon began throwing things around the room and when Sal tried to get him to stop, Dillon pulled a knife and threatened Sal. Dillon did put the knife down when the other boys confronted him, but anger overwhelmed Wayne and he punched Dillon in the face.

The result of this sordid incident was that Dillon left that night and did not finish the semester. His father filed restraining orders against Wayne and Sal. The one against Sal was dropped, but Wayne, who handled the situation on his own despite his parents' offer to help, was suspended from school for a semester and is not sure what happened to Dillon.

Wayne believes his school was wrong to suspend him. It was Dillon, Wayne said, who threatened with a weapon, while he merely punched the guy. While rules and regulations are available for anyone who asks, most students and parents never learn of the rules until a student breaks one and faces punishment.

In the attempt to prevent matters from escalating to the degree it did between Wayne and Dillon, RAs generally receive training designed to address some of the more common adjustment problems. At Colorado State

University, for example, this includes instructions for putting on various "survival skill" programs in subjects such as managing finances, getting along with roommates, managing stress, and doing laundry. They also receive training in how to deal with diversity issues, eating disorders, and alcohol and drug use. And, since conflict resolution can be a major part of the job, RAs receive training in techniques for improving communication, negotiating compromise, and for some situations, working out contracts among the individuals involved in order to prevent future conflicts from becoming serious. If, however, a conflict becomes too prolonged or intense, it may be turned over to the hall director, and, in more extreme cases, students may be moved to different locations to settle things.

Sound impressive? It is and it should be because being an RA is a very demanding position for anyone. Keep in mind that RAs are often only one to three years older than the students they are supposed to mentor and monitor. They generally receive room and board for their efforts, but it is difficult to juggle their job and living situation. RAs are expected to develop a friendly relationship with the students on their floor while, at the same time, policing those students' behavior—to be responsible without being "a snitch." Duties can include putting in hours at the front desk, being available on-call for night duty once or twice per week, and conducting walk-throughs to check for problems and maintain a presence. These duties vary from school to school, as does the training provided, and, of course, the RAs themselves vary in their levels of skills and maturity. The ratio of RAs to residents can be as low as 1-to-9 or as high as 1-to-50. The school administration may be supportive of the RAs and hall directors in their efforts to enforce school policies by providing adequate resources and follow-through, or may undermine them by doing the opposite. Since student retention is a major concern in terms of school funding, there may be increasing pressure for the residence hall staff to fix the problem early, before it results in notifying parents or calling police.

In short, this is part of college life where expectations may exceed what is really possible, and where situations vary not only from school to school but also from residence hall to residence hall. Ask yourself a few questions: Should RAs provide seminars on doing laundry? Managing finances? Conflict resolution? Is that what most parents expect of them? Maybe not most, but in reality, a sufficient proportion of parents do hold such expectations, or else have not given the matter much thought; therefore, the need exists. Unless, of course, the student takes the option one RA described of two young women who packaged up their laundry every two weeks and sent it home to their mothers via UPS. Can anyone legitimately expect that an RA, who is also a full-time student, effectively and consistently carry out all of these responsibilities single-handedly? Hall directors and administrative staff from three of Colorado's state universities report receiving two to three calls per week, on average, from parents asking about their student's attendance and grades, how they're getting along with their roommates, whether they are drinking or taking drugs. Since it is not uncommon for a single residence hall to house more than three hundred students, and since privacy laws forbid divulging information about legal adults eighteen years and older, it is unreasonable to expect hall directors or RAs to answer such questions from parents.

What schools can do, and many have done, is to look for ways in which they can assist students in their transition process while also creating a more "user-friendly" environment. For example, some campus police, once having been called into a situation by an RA, will make an effort to focus any enforcement actions on themselves, rather than the RA. The campus police try to portray the RA as a friend who was concerned or trying to help—someone who is looking out for the student's welfare rather than looking to bust the rule breakers—with the intent to encourage other students to report to the RA when there is a problem. Police also often play a major role in developing and presenting tour materials and orientation programs, and oftentimes these efforts are designed to dovetail with RA training.

Here again is more evidence of the importance of attending school orientation programs. Not only will parents and students learn about important security and health services information, but orientation sessions also provide insights into just how seriously a school views safety issues. School Web sites often provide schedules or programs from a recent or upcoming orientation, so even while still in the school researching process, a parent has the option of comparing security policies. As part of its orientation materials, the Crime Prevention Office of the University of Northern Colorado Police Department presents a peer-facilitated seminar entitled "Stop, Look, and Listen," which offers information on a variety of health and safety issues to freshman, while a similar, but separate presentation is provided to parents. The program includes five segments:

- "Who Let the Dawgs Out?" addresses issues of sexual assault on campus. Discussion topics include the difference between sexual assault and rape, stranger versus acquaintance sexual assault, the role of alcohol in sexual assault, laws concerning the reporting of sexual assault cases, and preventing sexual assault.
- "Sex in the City" addresses attitudes toward sexual assault issues. Through group interactions, students are asked to react to a number of commonly held myths concerning sexual assault, then participate in discussions in which these myths are corrected. For example, students often assume that isolated areas with trees and bushes are the most likely place for a sexual assault to occur on campus. In fact, since acquaintance sexual assault is much more common than stranger assault, students are more likely to be victimized in a dorm room than in an isolated area.
- "The Good, the Bad, and the Ugly" deals with sexually transmitted diseases and prevention, with particular focus on health services available on campus, protection, and how to get help if a student suspects she or he might be infected.
- "Hollywood Squares at UNC" uses a game-show format to encourage discussions about alcohol and drug use issues.
- "10 Things I Hate About You" is a small group exercise to help teach assertive communication. Participants are presented with the basic dynamics of assertive communication, then work in groups to prepare assertive responses to questions as varied as cheating on exams to protecting a friend from a dangerous party situation to addressing roommate conflicts.

Schools also have experimented with various residence hall policies and programs, such as placing students in particular residence halls based on common interests or majors in an effort to create greater compatibility and an atmosphere in which new friendships can blossom. In some cases, schools are going further in that direction and designing school "communities" by integrating housing areas with classrooms, faculty offices, and graduate student or faculty apartments. Coed housing also has been popular for some time now, though in some circles still controversial. Some schools also offer alcohol- and drug-free dorms, bans that apply even if any of the students living in the hall are of legal age for alcohol use. Again, parents and their students can research these options before selecting a school and/or residence hall, but be ready to choose a dorm soon after the acceptance letter arrives since housing placements are generally done on a first come, first served basis.

Legal rights and privacy

"I can't wait until I'm eighteen. Then I can do whatever I want!"

How many parents have heard that? When those young adults do turn eighteen, some actually get up and leave home, but most stay put until they graduate from high school and find a job that pays enough for them to afford rent, or until they go to college where they continue to rely on parents for emotional, and at least partially, financial support. But they are right about turning eighteen; at that point they no longer need parental permission for much of anything. No need for you to sign that line that reads, "If under eighteen, parent or guardian signature." Those eighteen-year-olds are now legal adults and with that comes a wave of not only rights and responsibilities, but also of privacy benefits.

Captain Bob Chaffee of the Colorado State University Police Department often finds himself dealing with parents who ask for help that he cannot provide.

"Parents will call a hall director because they can't get in touch with their son or daughter," Chaffee said. "The director does a welfare check with neighboring students and any friends they might know of, but sometimes they can't find out anything useful from that, so they call us. We start an investigation, and oftentimes find out that the student has moved in with a friend, or gone on a trip without telling their folks. Then all we can do is encourage the student to call home. It's up to them."

Chaffee said that even if he or his officers find that a student has been in an accident and is hospitalized, all they can do is refer the parent to the appropriate institutions, which, in turn, are restricted by HIPAA (Health, Information, Portability and Accountability Act). This is also true for students in detox.

"On the other hand," Chaffee continued, "the laws are there for protection purposes and sometimes this is very important. There may be times when there is a restraining order against a family member or another individual coming into contact with a student. That student has a right to be protected, and that's part of our responsibility and the school's responsibility."

Dona Johnson, administrative assistant for the University of Northern Colorado's Sociology Department, has had similar experiences to Chaffee. "Every semester there are a few times when a parent calls us and asks questions about their student," Johnson explained. "They ask whether their student is attending class, or how their midterms went, or whether they've dropped a class. We can't answer those questions—we are only allowed to give out public information available online without the student's password. The parents can get pretty angry about it, but there's nothing we can do for them."

The two major pieces of federal legislation that protect privacy are the Family Education Rights and Privacy Act (FERPA) and the Health, Information, Portability, and Accountability Act (HIPAA). Health-care providers, including those on college campuses, are bound by HIPAA stipulations, while colleges and universities are bound by FERPA stipulations that apply to both academic and disciplinary matters. In addition, state legislation may further restrict release of various kinds of information, with specific restrictions differing from state to state.

What this means for parents is that they have limited, if any, access to their student's school, health, credit, or disciplinary records without the student's written consent. There are exceptions—generally involving drug or alcohol use—in which schools are allowed to inform the parents, but again, schools vary widely in terms of specific policies for doing so. At the University of Northern Colorado, for example, parents may be notified if a student has two violations involving alcohol or drug use, but if the violation is deemed serious, parents may be notified with the first violation. Other campuses, however, may be more reluctant to contact parents without the student's consent. In interviews with RAs, housing administrators, parent-school liaison officers, campus police, counselors, health-care providers, academic departmental staff, and faculty, stories abound of the difficulties in explaining a situation to a worried and/or angry parent whose questions cannot be answered. What tends to grate parents the worst is the fact that these restrictions hold even if they are paying all or most of the bills. The laws give no rights to the check writer—they only take the student's age into account.

Elizabeth, whom we met in Chapter 6, well remembers the phone call she received at the end of October of her son Tim's freshman year at Fort Lewis College. "I got a phone call from Tim's roommate, Chase," Elizabeth said. "He was in the emergency room at the hospital in Durango (Colorado). The first thing Chase said to me was, 'Don't worry, Tim is in good hands.'"

Eager for skiing to begin, Tim, Chase, and some other friends had taken their backcountry skis into the mountains near Durango. It was early in the season, and a jump and a bad fall on too little snow left Tim with a compression fracture in his back. In great pain and unable to move, Tim had to rely on his friends to get him out of the mountains and to the hospital. From there, Chase, a premed student, relayed information to Elizabeth, who lived an eight-hour drive away.

"After Chase told me what happened, I asked if Tim could walk," Elizabeth remembered. "Chase said: 'They're working on it right now.' Then Chase told me they would be taking Tim in for an MRI and that he was in too much pain to talk to me.

Chase said he would call again as soon as he knew more."

Elizabeth immediately got on the Internet to glean phone numbers and information about the hospital. Although Chase called Elizabeth later that evening, and even though she spoke once to Tim who was "out of it" on morphine, Elizabeth was surprised that no doctors or anyone from the hospital called. The next morning she called the hospital and spoke with a nurse who told Elizabeth she could not give any information about Tim because of HIPAA privacy laws. Growing a bit agitated, Elizabeth asked to speak to the doctor who attended Tim. Although the nurse handed the phone over to the doctor, she told Elizabeth that he wouldn't be able to give her information either.

"When the doctor got on the phone, he basically said 'Screw HIPAA,'" Elizabeth said. "He said that if he had an eighteen-year-old son in the hospital somewhere, he hoped someone would give him information." The doctor assured Elizabeth that because Tim was young, he would heal and recover quickly.

Although Tim was well treated, logistical difficulties started immediately. Tim needed to leave the hospital, but he needed recovery care that he couldn't get in his dorm room. He ended up at a friend's house for a few days. Then Elizabeth wanted a second opinion about Tim's back. The hospital wouldn't release Tim's x-rays until he signed for them, but Tim was physically unable to get to the hospital for a couple of weeks. Elizabeth and her husband finally made it to Durango three weeks after the accident. "We should have gone immediately and helped him," Elizabeth said in hindsight. Now she strongly advises parents with college students: "Go to the local hospital and have your child sign information release forms before anything happens."

Agreeing with Elizabeth, Jeanette Rampone Gulder, corporate compliance coordinator for Poudre Valley Hospital (PVH) in Fort Collins, Colorado, said that parents should arrange for health information disclosure before they drop their students off at college. Gulder explained that HIPAA mandates that only the patient, or a person authorized and designated by the patient, has access to records and medical information. "So, if a student comes in unconscious, the student is treated and the hospital tries to contact relatives," Gulder said. "But the hospital cannot give out information unless that student has verbally okayed it or is carrying a card that authorizes someone else to receive that information. Even if you are paying a bill, or paying the insurance, you cannot receive medical information about the patient unless some authorized consent has already been given."

Gulder went on to say that if a parent comes into the hospital with identification and insurance information for the patient, it is up to the care provider to decide how much information to disclose. PVH wants to work with parents, Gulder said, but if the young adult wakes up and says he or she does not want the parents involved, it changes everything.

Although PVH offers medical release information forms that students can sign and keep on their person, not all hospitals do. Gulder strongly recommends that parents have a discussion with their college students about emergency hospital care before they leave for school and suggests that students carry some type of form that authorizes parents to receive information along with their insurance information.

Alcohol abuse

In addition to accidents such as the one Tim experienced skiing, students increasingly find themselves in difficult situations involving drug and alcohol use. In recent years, there have been a number of high-profile incidents in which students have died from alcohol poisoning, such as the tragic death of Samantha Spady at Colorado State University in 2004. Samantha drank between thirty and forty beer and vodka beverages in eleven hours and had a blood alcohol level (BAL) of 0.436 percent when she died (in the state of Colorado, a BAL of 0.08 percent is the legal limit for driving an automobile). It is a rare campus that does not send one or more students per week to a detox facility, often with BALs of 0.20 percent or more. Some students, particularly those who have established a pattern of drinking while still in high school, may have BALs as high as .30 or greater, which puts them at a high risk for alcohol poisoning.

As has been reported frequently in the popular press, oftentimes students are engaging in "binge drinking," generally defined as consuming five alcoholic drinks in one session or within a few hours. Since most are legally underage and cannot drink publicly, they may often "prime up" before going out—by chugging down a number of drinks before leaving home or a friend's apartment. While it must be remembered that many students do not drink, it still remains an area of concern.

Sabina had just left the stadium with her dad after watching the Colorado Buffs win a football game, but had said good-bye and was headed back to her dorm with some friends before going out to eat. As they approached the front steps of the dorm, they saw a girl they didn't know trying to drag Lyndsay, a friend of Sabina's, into the building. Lyndsay was unconscious and the other girl said she planned to get Lyndsay to her room and leave her there to sleep it off. Lyndsay had been drinking heavily at a party.

Sabina and her friends took Lyndsay to Sabina's room instead. Lyndsay came in and out of consciousness—when awake she was hysterical and vomiting and talked about random things. Sabina thought that if Lyndsay continued to vomit for a while she would be okay, but it wasn't long before Lyndsay completely lost her ability to hold up her head and talk, so Sabina and the others decided to call for help.

The girls first looked for an RA but couldn't find one, so they called 911. The operator asked questions about the girl's responsiveness. Did she respond to pain? Did she respond to water in her face? The answer was no to both.

When the ambulance came, Lyndsay was completely unconscious and her breathing had slowed to dangerous levels.

At the hospital, the nurse commented, "This is number 12 for the night," meaning that Lyndsay was the twelfth student brought in that night who had been drinking heavily.

The hospital took the relevant information about Lyndsay but stated that due to privacy restrictions, they could not give out information about her condition. Sabina knew Lyndsay's parents, so she called them and waited until Lyndsay's mother arrived. Sabina was at the hospital until about 3 a.m.

Later, Sabina discovered that Lyndsay had registered a BAL of .29 and had slipped in the bathroom at the party she had attended and injured her head. The combination of alcohol and the injury had made the situation quite serious, impairing her ability to walk or read for the following two weeks.

Sabina said, "It was lucky that we happened by at that time." She also noted that there seemed to be a fine line between when to call for help and when not to. She also became aware of a protection policy—that if an individual who is an underage drinker, or has been using drugs, calls in help for a friend in danger with alcohol or drugs, the police will not arrest the reporting individual.

A high school friend was visiting Chad and some other freshmen at Virginia Tech during Chad's freshman year. "We wanted to impress him with big partying," Chad said, and so the drinking began. Although underage, Chad said it was quite easy to get a fake ID and use it to buy beer in local grocery stores. "It was particularly easy if you had an out-of-state ID, which I had," Chad said. Chad admitted he drank between 10 and 15 beers over a five-hour period, then "bonged" two or three beers right before he went to bed. Chad is a sleepwalker, and the heavy dose of alcohol didn't slow him down that night. Like many dorm dwellers, Chad had a raised bed. When his sleepwalking took over, Chad stepped off his bed, hit his roommate's desk, and fell into the closet, hitting several objects. "I didn't wake up," Chad said, "but I was bleeding pretty badly. I know, because I followed the blood trail the next day." Chad figures he wandered around the halls in his sleep, but either no one saw him or no one came to his aid. He eventually wandered back to his bed.

The next day, Chad figured out what had happened. He remembers there was a big football game that day, but because his head was hurting, he decided to stay in his dorm room. "Some of my friends offered to take me to the hospital, but I told them to go to the game and have a good time," Chad said. "I tried to watch the game, but I felt so bad that after about 20 minutes I called an ambulance for myself." Chad required seven stitches below one eye, had a broken nose, and suffered a fractured cheekbone. "I learned my lesson," Chad said. "It was stupidity on my part."

Despite the personal consequence of drinking, Chad says he still drinks, but quickly points out that he has never drunk to such excess since his accident. Sabina said her friend Lyndsay also continues to drink, even after her near-fatal experience. Despite the numerous tragic stories involving college students and gluttonous amounts of drinking, many college students are attracted to, and can always find, those parties where the alcohol flows. Those students usually are aware of the health risks, but often they do not consider other risks that arise when alcohol is present. Of major concern to campus security, and, of course, to families, is that many sexual assault situations involve alcohol and/or drug use. Detective Slack of the University of Northern Colorado said, "When students have been drinking they sometimes bring home someone they don't really know, including into the dorms. We'll have cases where the young woman comes in with a guy from a party, asks his name so he can be checked in at the front desk, then takes him to her room. In that situation we have a guy that even she doesn't know who is in the dorm."

Consequences

Students who have exhibited persistent behavioral problems may be placed on probation, depending on the behaviors involved and school policies concerning disciplinary actions. If the problems are sufficiently serious, the student may be suspended, as happened to Wayne in the earlier story, but this again varies widely between schools. Generally, probationary policies include some form of agreement or contract between the student and the school concerning the terms for remaining enrolled. The degree of access parents have to this process, however, is limited under FERPA and subject to specific school policies.

Students and their parents also need to be aware of the relationship between school police and local community law enforcement, since students live and move about in both jurisdictions. In some communities, city police work directly with campus authorities in situations that involve students but occur off-campus. Generally these are cases of assault, sexual assault, underage drinking, drug offenses, driving violations, noise violations, and property damage situations. This could mean that if a student is cited or arrested by local police, the infraction also may be entered in the student's disciplinary record with the school and included in considerations for dismissal. While students often take exception to this, viewing it as a violation of privacy, the practice may well be legally established in a particular community and, therefore, no amount of complaining or threatening to call in the family attorney is likely to alter the practice or improve the student's position. On the other hand, a school or community may take a more lenient and less intrusive approach, primarily based on the argument that anyone eighteen years of age or older is an adult and, therefore, no reporting to the school is warranted. In turn, the school probably will not report disciplinary or legal infractions to the student's family.

How many times have I told you?

One point that should be clear is that the students must take some responsibility for their own personal safety and health. To repeat, schools are institutions. No matter how many resources schools devote to security services, to redesigning residence halls, or to creating orientation materials, they cannot fully compensate for the fact that some students seem to arrive at school unaware of the need to handle themselves responsibly, unaware that bad things can, in fact, happen to them. As Detective Slack stated earlier, the creation of a community setting, such as in a dorm, does not mean students can let down their defenses.

As Hadar and her roommate, Jessie, walked up to their dorm, they noticed an RA angrily telling a young man he must leave. Once the RA was inside, Hadar and Jessie asked the man, who looked only a few years older than they, what was going on. He told them the RA was being "mean" to him—that all he wanted to do was try to sell magazines to the students. Selling magazines was how he supported himself and he didn't think it was fair that they blocked him from "making his living."

Hadar and Jessie felt sorry for the guy, so they snuck him up to their dorm room. The girls got him a Coke and started chatting. After a while, the girls started feeling a bit uncomfortable. The man did not talk about his magazines and he showed no sign of leaving. Finally the man approached the girls and physically subdued Jessie. Hadar managed to get out of the room and down the hall where she recruited some male students to help. The students overwhelmed the man and threw him out. Hadar and Jessie never reported the incident.

Hadar did, however, tell her mother, Sara, about the encounter with the magazine salesman. Sara was appalled that Hadar and Jessie could be so naïve. Hadn't she taught Hadar, from the time she was a little girl, to stay away from strangers? Regardless of what parents teach their children when they are small, there is probably more preparation needed, or at least some review, when those children reach that wise age of fifteen or sixteen. How do parents begin the process of preparing their teenagers to take responsibility for their safety?

First, parents can take a look at the degree to which they are proactive in the area of security. Do you leave valuables exposed on the seat of your car in a parking lot? Do you lock doors at night? Are you involved in any public safety programs, such as Neighborhood Watch? Do you insist that Sarah or Josh wait in a safe place to be picked up from a school event? Do you keep informed of current drug use patterns among teenagers? Do you obey traffic laws and alcohol consumption laws? The idea is not that Mom and Dad "play cop" all the time, but rather role model for their teens, demonstrate that they take security issues seriously, and explain why they do so whenever it's appropriate.

Second, parents can give their teenager "graduated responsibilities." Through the junior high and high school years, Sarah and Josh could be allowed to stay out later, spend more time at their friends' homes, or spend time in group activities with no adult supervisor. If parents are afraid of turning their teenager loose, it could come back to haunt them once their legal adult leaves home.

Maryann earned the title "helicopter mom" because she controlled everything about her kids' comings and goings. Maryann insisted that her high school–age son, Nick, and his friends always come to her house for band practice, or to eat, to study, to party, to do whatever. Maryann wanted to know where Nick was at all times. She would grill Nick's friends on what was going on in the other kids' lives. If she heard that one of Nick's friends cut class or was drinking at a party, she would immediately call the friend's parents and tell them what happened. Maryann was so successful at watching over Nick that he never experimented with alcohol or drugs—quite the accomplishment in today's world.

When Nick went to college 2,000 miles from home, however, he was suddenly released from Maryann's protective watch. Nick became a "booze hound," a big partier. His grades slipped and a drinking problem emerged. Nick returned to his hometown after his lackluster freshman year, eventually graduated from college, but is unhappy and doesn't know what to do with his life. Even now, he has trouble making decisions.

The keys during the graduated responsibility process are that parents set clear boundaries and that the teen continually demonstrates that he will, in fact, follow whatever rules the parents set; call when he is supposed to call; and avoid situations he is supposed to avoid. Whenever they fail to do so, which will happen more than once, there should be consequences appropriate to the seriousness of the situation. If Sarah or Josh gets caught at an unsupervised party, is caught with alcohol or marijuana, or gets a speeding ticket and his or her parents regard it as "understandable given the peer pressure my child was under," or "not that serious since no one was injured," or "the city's fault for not putting out more warning signs," then what do Sarah and Josh learn? They learn that Mom or Dad will come to the rescue; therefore, there is no reason for Sarah and Josh to watch out for themselves or respect the rules.

Another possibility is to find out what kind of resources your student's high school offers. Many high schools offer peer counseling or conflict resolution workshops. Your student may have participated in a program that focuses on peer communication skills, conflict resolution, or something similar without your knowing it because often such programs are built into special classes mandated by the school. Unfortunately, students often consider these classes "lame," but the hope is that they come away with recognition of how to peacefully resolve problems.

Always consider the vast amount of information on the Internet in your efforts to steer your teenager toward making responsible safety decisions. One worthy Web site, http://www.factsontap.org/index. htm, offers an alcohol and drug education, prevention, and intervention program for both college and high school students. The programs, Facts on

Tap and Transitions, are broken into components for students, parents, and health professionals.

In teaching teenagers about personal safety, the trick is to find a balance: to be proactive about security without being paranoid—in which case the teen views the parent as way out of touch with reality—and to be the responsible freedom guide without coming down too hard. It is important to remember that in order to actually be a more responsible young adult, the teen needs opportunities to develop good decision-making skills—and that means facing the consequences of his or her mistakes.

Preparing Your Teenager: Keeping Them Safe and Handing Over Responsibilities

Teaching teenagers safety and responsibility is tricky at best. They are at the stage where rebellion, of some degree, is normal. The best way to prepare your teenager is to model safe, responsible behavior yourself and to set clear expectations and consequences.

1) Model and insist upon behavior that will keep your teenager safe.

Challenge	Solution
You grew up in a rural area where few people locked buildings or cars. You tend to do the same, but lately your teenager has noticed and is asking why you don't lock the door.	As you already know, our children pay more attention to what they see or hear us do as opposed to what we tell them to do. Model behavior that your teenager will need to emulate once she leaves home. Lock the doors to your house when you leave and lock your car doors. Be sure she sees you doing this and admit to her that you had gotten careless.

Challenge	Solution
Your freshman teenager is excited about going to the homecoming dance her first year in high school. She is going with a group of friends and says she will call you when it is time to pick her up. She says her friends have talked about walking to a coffee shop after the dance.	Now that she is in high school, your teenager is expecting looser restrictions. If you haven't already, you need to make it clear what you expect when she goes out. Will she have a set curfew or will it change according to the circumstance? Make it clear that you need to know where she is at all times—that if she changes locations, she needs to call first and ask. Emphasize that this is for your peace of mind and her safety. Ask her what time the dance is finished. If she doesn't know, check the school Web site or call the school to find out. Ask where the coffee shop is located and the route they plan to take. If you are not comfortable with the location, the route, or the time, be clear about your expectations. Consider suggesting that you pick up her and her friends and take them to the coffee shop. Discuss your concerns, listen to her ideas, but be firm about your decision. Appoint a specific time and place to pick her up, and have consequences ready if she fails to comply.

Challenge	Solution
You know your teenager was at a party last night. You weren't comfortable with the situation surrounding the party, but you gave in with a stated curfew. Your teenager came home on time, but in the morning, you find an empty beer can in the trunk of the car she drove. She claims it was not her beer and that she did not drink and drive. She points out that you always drive after having a beer or glass of wine at a restaurant, and how would it be any different if she had drunk the beer?	You have caught her with some evidence, but she also has made a valid point. First, point out that she is underage; therefore, having the beer is breaking the law. Second, stress how dangerous it is to drink and drive under any circumstance. Then own up to her point that you drive home after having an alcoholic beverage at a restaurant. If you want to model safe and lawful behavior, at this point, you should make a vow to your teenager and yourself that you will not drive after drinking at a restaurant. Alternatives include purchasing a portable breath tester that will allow you to measure your alcoholic intake, determine if you need to take a cab, or have a designated driver available. Make sure she sees that you have changed your behavior.

2) Give your teenager graduated responsibilities.

Challenge	Solution
Your high school sophomore worries you. He doesn't tell you his plans, he comes home later than you think he should, and he is vague about where he has been. You ground him occasionally, but nothing seems to work.	Consider starting from scratch. Have you made your rules and consequences clear? If not, it is time to do so. Write down the rules for curfews, party limitations, and communication requirements. For example, state that you must talk with an adult that will

Challenge	Solution
	be at the party he attends, that he must ask permission to attend activities, that he must be available by phone, and that he must inform you of any change in plans in advance. Also write down the corresponding consequences for violations. They could involve missing an upcoming event or loss of privileges such as driving, cell phone, or computer or television time. Discuss the rules and consequences with him and let him give input. Explain to him that if he follows the rules—showing responsibility—that you will revisit the rules in the future and give him more autonomy over his free time. Follow through.
You made rules clear for your teenager from the time he started middle school. For the most part he has made curfew, called you when his plans changed, and acted responsibly in most situations. Now he is seventeen years old and wants to stay overnight at his best friend's condo at a ski area that is a two-hour drive away. It would be just the two of them, as the friend's parents will not be there.	Ultimately, you must feel comfortable with the situation. But consider that this is a good opportunity for him to really prove himself. First, speak with the friend's parents and discuss the plan with them. If you decide to let him go, make the rules clear. He must call you as soon as he reaches the condo, at agreed upon times while he is skiing, and again when they start home. Be clear that there is to be no party, alcohol, or drugs. When he returns home after following your rules, be sure to praise him for being responsible.

Challenge	Solution
You have made the rules clear since your teenager started middle school. Now that he is a junior in high school, he argues that your rules are too strict and that you need to loosen up and let him make more of his own decisions. He has followed the rules pretty well in the past.	Be open to his ideas. His respect of your rules shows that he is ready for more responsibility. Consider extending his curfew or eliminating it entirely, making that decision per each particular activity. Give him more autonomy in deciding what he does with his time. Explain to him that you want him to be safe and that you trust him to let you know about his plans in general. If major changes occur, he should still contact you, but he probably doesn't need to tell you every step he takes. Your trust in him will help grow his responsibility even further.
After many arguments, your teenager wears you down enough that you agree he can attend a party that doesn't sound "right" to you. You give him a curfew and name the consequences if he doesn't make it. You also remind him: no alcohol or drugs. He does not have a good track record following rules, and again he comes home forty-five minutes late, did not answer his cell phone when you called, and smells heavily of marijuana.	If you do not want to speak to him when he comes in, ask for his car keys and tell him what time the discussion will take place in the morning. Have him repeat what was expected of him. Regardless of his explanation, he has proven himself irresponsible. Explain to him that until he can show responsible and lawful behavior, he will be more restricted. Remind him of the consequences and follow through. Be sure to keep your eyes open for situations in which he does show responsibility and praise him for those, telling him that if he continues in that vein, he will have fewer rules and restrictions.

Remember to first look at your own behaviors and make any adjustments that show you operate responsibly, safely, and within the law. If your teenager is taking dangerous risks and you feel overwhelmed, look for outside help to guide you and give you ideas. Despite how hard it is, follow through with consequences when your teenager defies the rules—if you don't, other authorities eventually will. Reward your teenager for responsible behavior by granting her more "freedoms," then enjoy the freedom and relief it is for you!

Chapter 8

The Emotional Roller Coaster:
Loneliness and Emotional Support

Excitement and anticipation build as your teenager prepares to leave for college. You may leave him at the dorm with tears in your eyes, but you are certain that this exhilarating change in his life will carry him through the ups and downs he may encounter. You may be right, but don't be too sure. Parents need to recognize that although their teenagers longed for this move and new chapter in their lives, it will present emotions that they probably didn't expect and are not sure how to handle. Parents need to offer support, a listening ear, and encouragement to their new college students.

As new freshmen, Melissa and her roommate had moved into the dorm early during the week before classes were to start. Best to get settled in a few days in advance, they thought; meet some new people, get things organized, become familiar with their surroundings. They and their parents had visited the dorm in July, so they had arrived with some items they knew they needed or wanted: area rugs, posters that could be mounted without making nail holes in the walls, and their favorite pillows.

Jana, Melissa's mother, was therefore "mystified" to find that for their first two weeks, Melissa and her roommate had not eaten a single meal in the dorm cafeteria. Never mind that it was just down the hall from their room, was generally considered one of the best dorm cafeteria options on campus, and afforded one of the most obvious opportunities to meet people. "It's too gross!" Melissa said.

Melissa's parents had spent a few hundred dollars on a semester meal card, assuming it would cover nearly all of her eating expenses other than the occasional pizza or hamburger. So why wasn't she using it? Even more perplexing was the fact that the girls' alternative strategy had been to live almost solely on the stash of peanut butter, bread, and orange juice provided by the roommate's mother, "for snacks." Once that had been depleted, the girls had used their spending money to buy more of the same, plus cheese, lunch meat, and chips. They also seemed to be spending nearly all their free time in their room or that of another friend from high school who lived down the hall. What was going on?

Day by day, during the frequent phone conversations between mother and daughter, the situation became clear. The girls, in spite of their best intentions otherwise, hunkered down in their room and did not leave the building except to go to classes. Not only that, but Melissa related some fairly disconcerting stories to her mother about other young women in the dorm—some seemingly disoriented, some vomiting as the result of their anxiety, others virtually pacing the halls wondering how they would ever adjust to the "sardine can" existence into which they had gotten themselves. As for eating in the cafeteria, Melissa felt that the prospect of facing ninety or a hundred new people at dinner was just too overwhelming. Jana began to realize that while the girls were indeed attempting to expand their horizon, they needed to do it an inch or two at a time.

In the same way that the issue of personal safety has to be viewed with some degree of balance, the more general issue of transitioning into college life, in all its aspects, requires the same kind of effort. There are various and wide-ranging adjustments that students have to make, which were discussed in previous chapters. Students need to adjust to the campus life social scene and safety risks, the new and/or different academic requirements, the need to take on new responsibilities, and more. Does this mean that they will inevitably indulge in drug or alcohol use? That they will put on the "freshman 15," the pounds many freshmen unwittingly gain due to ample dorm food? That they will develop eating disorders such as anorexia or bulimia? These questions seriously concern parents and students.

Shanna, a sophomore at the University of Northern Colorado, was visiting her boyfriend, Michael, a student at the University of Michigan. "We went to the student center for coffee," she said, "and to get warm because it was raining and windy outside. I went into the restroom and there was this long row of stalls, and on each stall door there was a sign, a notice taped on the door. It said: 'If you are purging, call this number,' followed by the telephone number of a counseling hotline for students."

At first, Shanna had been tempted to think of this as more ammunition in the "my school is better than your school" dialogue she and Michael had been having. Then she remembered the Wednesday afternoon when she had been in a restroom on her own campus and had seen a young woman exit a stall after a session of vomiting. "Are you okay?" she had asked, thinking the girl was ill with the flu or something similar. She received a quick reply, "I'm fine." The young woman then proceeded to pick up her purse and book bag and head out the restroom door, in the direction of a nearby classroom. Shanna noticed how thin she appeared.

When students go to college, whether they continue living at home or live on campus, they are entering a period of intellectual and emotional stimulation. Dr. Robert Portnoy, director of counseling and psychological services at the University of Nebraska, tells parents that during college, students may "forge new identities, or seek to clarify their values and beliefs." They may, he warns, "question or challenge the values you (the parents) hold dear." These changes may occur quickly, and some students may feel in over their heads and confused about how to cope with their experiences. At other times, they may discover that they are resilient and capable in ways that surprise both them and their family. College students are asked to become full-fledged adults and to complete their educational goals at the same time. They will need space as well as continued contact with family, the freedom to make their own mistakes, but with the knowledge that they have the support and encouragement of their parents.

The son of immigrants from Mexico, Octavio was a first-generation college student who lived at home, about an hour's drive from the small college he attended in California. Octavio's father expected him to be home every weekend to work in the family's construction business. His father continually asked Octavio to leave college and work full time, insisting that Octavio's help was more important than school. Octavio tried to continue with his studies, but the lack of support from home proved to be overwhelming. Octavio finished the semester with a 3.0 GPA and withdrew from school to work full time with his father. He said he did not want to let his family down.

How do parents "let go" of these young people and provide them the support that they may need at the same time? In general, there are four major points to address: (1) loneliness and/or homesickness is normal; (2) transitioning takes time, and different students are on different timetables; (3) expectations, of both student and parent, can play a major role in shaping the transitioning experience; and (4) the role of the parent needs to be one of support and a listening ear, not one who will rescue or instruct.

Loneliness is normal

At most college orientation programs, loneliness is one of the first issues addressed with incoming students and their parents. Nearly all new students will, at some point, feel lonely and out of sync with the social networks around them, feel homesick for their own bedroom, their old friends, even their siblings and parents. In a way, this expectation of feeling homesick or lonely may seem an odd assumption. In today's world, where many families have experienced major transitions such as relocations to different parts of the country, divorce, and remarriage, one could argue that as a society we have become accustomed to change and readjustment as a part of everyday life. Parents may have a tendency to think, "no big deal," as their high school student transforms into the college student.

As students look toward their first semester, they often see only the potential freedoms they have been craving while living at home: eat what you want and when you want, sleep until noon or later, start homework at midnight on the day before it's due, ditch a class if you feel like it, go to parties or hang out on school nights, and, best of all, no parents asking where you're going and when you'll be home. The parents, who have been watching as their son or daughter excitedly packs up iPods, headphones, laptop computers, and new clothes, may assume that with all the potential opportunities for new friends and activities, their student will not have time to be lonely. That, however, is often not the case, in the past or now.

Dr. Portnoy of the University of Nebraska told this story of the former Boston Celtics star Larry Bird. Larry was from the small town of French Lick, Indiana, where his basketball talent was discovered by college recruiters. Larry's family struggled financially, so the scholarship offer in 1974 from Indiana University, considered to have one of the top college basketball programs at the time, was Larry's ticket to higher education. The move to the big campus and city life of Bloomington proved too much for the shy, small-town Larry. Intimidated and overwhelmed by the size of the campus and the unfamiliar "cosmopolitan" lifestyle, Larry felt estranged and homesick. He holed up in his dorm room to avoid the alien world of the campus and finally retreated to home after one month at the school.

The story of Larry Bird, of course, had a positive ending. Once back in French Lick, he worked for the town's street department and other odd jobs, before feeling brave enough to try school once more. He chose Indiana State University, a smaller school that felt less cosmopolitan and less overwhelming. He learned to adjust, led the school's basketball team to thrilling seasons, and the rest is history.

Obviously, a certain amount of disorientation and loneliness may be inevitable, but the situation need not be as difficult and disorienting as Larry Bird experienced. Those first few days or weeks may be a bit less intimidating if Mom and Dad provide some reassuring, but measured, support.

Leah was certain that she would be just fine. Her mother, Julie, had come with her from Seattle, the two of them arriving at the University of Illinois in time for the last orientation program before the beginning of fall semester. After two days of getting acquainted with Leah's new surroundings and after making sure that she was settled in and feeling comfortable with her new roommate, Julie left for home.

However, in spite of Leah's protests that "things are all fine, Mom," Julie and her husband, Jeff, followed a prearranged plan to offer support to their oldest, and somewhat stubborn, daughter. Every two or three days, during the first four weeks of the semester, they would call Leah. These calls were unscheduled, often brief, just "touching base." Gradually, hesitantly, Leah began to confide that her roommate was drinking heavily on the weekends, coming in late, and waking her up with long and loud stories about her evening, her boyfriend back home, and her ideas for the future. Not all of Leah's classes were as exciting as she had hoped they would be, and, in fact, one professor actually read from his notes in a monotone. She'd only succeeded in making one new friend from her dorm.

Julie and Jeff listened sympathetically. After listening they sometimes retold the stories of their own similar experiences when they had been in school, talking about how those experiences had felt. Then they listened some more. They also suggested some possible actions Leah might take. Could she, for example, work on negotiating some ground rules with her roommate? Could she view the monotoned professor as a singular and unlucky experience rather than proclaiming all philosophy teachers boring? Could she and her new friend make it a goal to find another new friend and organize a night out for pizza or a movie together? Finally, they reminded Leah that when she had changed high schools at the beginning of her junior year, she had felt totally disconnected. It took, however, only a few weeks for her to make new friends. "This is much harder," Julie said. "You are a long way from home and you can't come home to your own family at night. But you really have done some of this before; maybe you could try to remember that. Most of all, you need to give it some time."

Janet Fritz, with Colorado State University's Department of Human Development and Family Studies, said that one of the most important things parents can do is provide emotional support in a way that keeps the communication channels open, allowing the student to admit that things may not be going quite as planned. "Be a sympathetic listener," she recommended, "but also be optimistic. Encourage them to look for solutions or to look at their own strengths that will help them make the transition." Similarly, parents can encourage their teens to set small goals for themselves, such as the new-friend-plus-pizza idea Julie suggested. Too shy or nervous to pedal to the biking club's meeting? Okay, then maybe you could just call and ask for more information about their activities. Don't feel comfortable going to the pool to swim laps? Maybe you can find someone to go with you, or else just go to the pool, find out when it is open, and check the layout of the locker room. Having trouble meeting people? Try going to one of the activities organized by the dorm staff. And yes, it may seem lame to do that, but, on the other hand, the students attending are there because they specifically want to meet people, and it is a start. Inch by inch, yard by yard, the comfort zone will expand.

Dr. Fritz also suggested another way in which parents can offer support, one that can easily be forgotten. "Students have mailboxes," she said. "And they really do like to find something in them, especially something from home." Letters, small packages, photos—all may be much appreciated while conveying the message that the students' family is there for them, even if, at this point, they are more in the background than was once the case.

The idea of sending such things through the mail may seem outdated in these days of electronic communication. It is, however, the underlying message that counts. Students are navigating their way through a new bureaucracy in which they are now known by their school ID number and are members of a student body that may be larger than all of the high schools in their hometown combined, perhaps even larger than the community in which they grew up. Their teachers generally will not know who they are until halfway through the semester or even later. So, what does your letter or package mean? Someone important to them took the time and effort to write a letter, wrap a package, clip a newspaper article, and mail it. That corny card from Dad, that package of your son's favorite hard candy, that article about your daughter's former soccer team, somehow brings a little bit of home—and comfort—to their new life.

Transitioning takes time

At the beginning of this chapter, Melissa and her roommate had been holing up in their dorm room, waiting for their comfort zone to expand. This, of course, was not the way they had pictured their first weeks at school. Was it unusual? Not as much as some might think. And in their case, it did not go on for the entire semester.

For nearly three weeks after Melissa's move into the dorm, her mother, Jana, had received at least one call per day from her daughter. In fact, there had been a number of days that included two or three calls. Then, one Friday night as she was getting ready for bed, Jana realized that there had been no calls from her daughter that day. The next afternoon, Jana called her sister, Pam. "Oh dear!" she exclaimed. "Melissa didn't call yesterday! I'm not sure what to think!"

"Jana," said Pam, "I think this is supposed to be a good thing, not a bad one. She's adjusting, feeling more comfortable. My guess is, you will hear from her less and less often."

"I know," said Jana. "It's just a little scary to realize this is actually happening. At least now maybe she'll eat something besides sandwiches and chips; go out and do some things that interest her. She's always had lots of friends, and always was busy coming and going, so much so that it was sometimes hard to keep track. I guess maybe now she's getting back into that mode."

In fact, Melissa was getting back into that mode. By midsemester she was spending time with new friends, learning how to successfully work with her teachers when there was a question or problem in class, and eating nearly all of her meals at one of the campus locations covered on her meal card. Best of all, she was feeling relieved. Unexpectedly, Melissa realized that she needed reassurance that her parents would still support her—and reassured she was. At the same time, she regained some of her earlier self-confidence. College life was not so overwhelming anymore. After all, in the past few years she had adjusted to a new high school, had taken classes at both a university and at a community college near her home while earning her high school diploma, and even had managed to secure a real estate license. As the dorm environment and her new neighbors became more familiar, as she began to associate this as her new "home base," Melissa began to refocus. Here she would be able to flex herself even further than she had before, explore her own ideas about her academic major and her future—and have some fun in the process.

Jody Donovan, assistant to the vice president of student affairs at Colorado State University, tells parents that it is not just the student going through a transition but the entire family, something Jana discovered as Melissa slowly gained confidence in her new environment. Donovan points to the three stages of transition as outlined by author William Bridges: (1) letting go, (2) the neutral zone, and (3) the new beginning. She explains that parents need to let go of their feelings of control, of their need to be involved in every part of their student's life, before they can celebrate the new beginning of the college experience with their student. She warns that while students are excited, conflicting emotions, such as sadness and uncertainty, can sweep through them. If a student gets stuck in uncertainty and fear, she can become stuck in the neutral zone, a place that can paralyze a confused student. The student needs to know she has a listening parent, who will be supportive even through the student's emotional roller-coaster rides.

Donovan says that the idea of letting go does not really sink in with most parents until the spring semester of their child's senior year in high school. Parents may sadly pronounce this as "the last spring break we'll have together," or "the last summer vacation we'll take as a family." In reality, that is most often not true, as families still gather for holidays and vacations. Grasping the idea that Josh or Sarah is about to leave home, though, is the important step. Donovan suggests that parents discuss the range of emotions that both they and their student might feel when the college separation begins. She also recommends journaling about those emotions during that last year in high school, and exposing your high school student to college students who have made the adjustment and who can offer encouragement to your teenager.

Expectations play a major role

Musing over the various experiences of students and their families in this and previous chapters, it is clear that the reality of the transition into college life is rarely as expected. It is easier or harder, riskier or safer, exciting or a letdown—whatever the reality, it often does not fit the image parents and students had in mind.

Phoebe and her parents had agreed on one thing: she definitely did not need her family to be involved when she moved away to school. She had already spent the summer away from home working at a mountain resort and sharing an apartment with friends. Besides, her older sister was an upperclassman at the same school and lived only a few blocks from campus, so she would be there in case Phoebe needed anything. In fact, Phoebe had helped her sister make the move two years earlier and since then had driven over on weekends for visits or day trips to go skiing. She already knew where the local hangouts were located, and she was going to room with a girl she knew from high school—not a close friend, but at least it made things predictable. Her roommate wouldn't move in until two days after Phoebe.

A few days before classes, and one day before the freshman placement exams, Phoebe's friend, Erika, borrowed the family pickup truck and the two girls loaded up Phoebe's things and headed out for the hour's drive to the school. Phoebe, who had not attended an orientation, had never seen her dorm complex, but her sister gave directions on how to get there. Mom waved good-bye from the front porch; Dad was still at work.

Phoebe's sister, Jacee, and one of her friends met Phoebe and Erika at the dorm. Both Jacee and her friend were anxious to help Phoebe unload as quickly as possible since they had just been invited to a party. Much of their conversation while lugging boxes and bags to Phoebe's room on the second floor consisted of speculation about what kind of party it would be and whether they would want to stay long. Phoebe was undaunted. This was to be her new beginning, her chance to make new friends, to redefine herself. Adrenaline was keeping up her spirits.

The four managed to get Phoebe checked in at the dorm office and the truck completely unloaded just before dark. Wishing Phoebe well, Jacee waved good-bye; just a few minutes later, Erika left. Phoebe was left sitting on the bed next to her boxes and wondering where she had packed her sheets. Her college experience had begun.

In less than half an hour, however, a feeling of fear and abandonment began to set in. While searching through her things, Phoebe could hear girls laughing and talking in rooms just down the hall. She assumed they were all good friends, and she felt too shy to go and introduce herself. She was hungry and thirsty, but she was unsure as to where the vending machines were and didn't want to stand out as someone who didn't know her way around.

Phoebe had the growing sense that her dreams of a carefree life away from home were crumbling. She had no idea who else from her high school was at the college and where they might be living, no idea if there was a nearby bank so she could set up a checking account, no idea where she was to report for placement exams, and only a vague idea about where the cafeteria, mailboxes, and lounge areas were. She was only sure of three things: she knew where the student center was, she knew when the dorm doors would be locked, and she knew with cold certainty that this move was going to be a lot more difficult than she had thought. She spent her first two nights in the dorm fighting back tears and wishing she'd stayed at home.

For families who have not been through it before, it is nearly impossible to anticipate just what it is going to be like for the new college freshman to make the move from home to college. In the story related above, both of Phoebe's parents had been to college, and yet they misjudged the possibilities. Many parents anticipate that their children will simply repeat their same experience in a contemporary setting, in spite of the fact that their son or daughter may have different coping skills than they had and are entering a different type of social scene than the parents remember. Conversely, parents who did not go to college, or who lived with their parents while attending a local school, may have formed images or expectations based on what they see as lost opportunities. They may, without realizing it, hold unrealistic expectations about what lies ahead for their son or daughter, and accordingly hold unrealistic expectations about how their son or daughter will respond. Thus, as mentioned earlier, school liaison offices tend to focus on the needs of families with little or no college experiences.

When expectations are not met, students may hide bad news from parents because they think something terrible will happen. How you handle that news sends strong messages to your student.

Declaring herself a bio-medical science major was almost a given for Martina. Both her parents were successful medical doctors and her sister was already in medical school. Martina was accepted into an accelerated program that would allow her to finish her undergraduate requirements in three years, then move the fourth year to medical school at UCLA, a program and career path her parents expected of her. Unfortunately, it was not the path Martina wanted for herself, but she was afraid to express that objection to her parents. She did not want to be a doctor and did not know what to do, knowing that such a declaration would disappoint her parents.

Martina made passing grades her first two years, but she was not qualified to stay in the bio-medical science program. Seeking someone's advice, Martina approached one of her biology professors who, impressed with Martina's attention to detail, had hired her during an earlier semester to work on his cancer research team. Martina told the professor how stressed she was that her family expected her to become a medical doctor. With Martina's approval, the professor called her father and told him that his daughter was a gifted researcher and that he wanted Martina to work with him for the next two years.

The professor also highly recommended that Martina follow the standard route to graduation instead of the bio-medical program. Feeling supported by her professor's faith in her research ability, Martina relaxed, did well academically, and graduated with honors. She continued cancer research and is happy in her field.

As this story hints, parents often feel that their children's success is a reflection of themselves. "Parents need to let go of that idea," Colorado State's Donovan says. "Some of our best lessons are learned through mistakes." The challenge for parents is to recognize that the expectations and images of college life they hold may be skewed by their own hopes and aspirations, or by other sources such as stories they've heard from friends, relatives, or the media. If parent and student are not communicating, the problem is made worse. If a teenager had an open, confiding relationship with her parents while at home, she will likely continue that openness while at school. If not, it is unlikely that she will begin confiding in her parents once at college.

Valerie came to college carrying a secret she had shared only with one of her closest friends. She was gay. In high school she had gone through the motions of dating, had pretended to be interested when boys took an interest in her, and had simply kept quiet when friends shared notes on their sexual activities. Her primary social strategy had been to present herself as a geek, a student too involved in studying and science projects to be interested in much of a social life. It was a strategy she had perfected over time, an effort she felt forced to undertake since not only did her parents strongly condemn homosexuality, but so did much of the small rural community where they lived. Her parents, on the other hand, fervently hoped college would make Valerie more social and that she would finally become more interested in finding a boyfriend.

Valerie loved music and dancing and dreamed of playing bass guitar in a band. She longed for the freedom to be more honest about her identity, to talk freely about her feelings, and to spend some time exploring the works of various writers and artists on the subject. Most of all, she wanted to find a way to feel "more normal."

Almost immediately after moving to campus, Valerie searched for the campus organization for gay, lesbian, bisexual, and transsexual students. She knew there was one because she had looked up the information online, but she needed to talk with someone in order to get a better sense of how this group functioned. In particular, she wanted to know whether group members had to be totally open about their sexual orientation. After two telephone conversations she made up her mind. The next day she found herself having coffee with one of the group members, and soon after that she was walking around campus with her new friends.

Then came the questions: Should she tell her parents? How could she? As she was learning from the experiences of others in the group, this wasn't going to be easy or predictable. Some parents had apparently handled the news reasonably well over time and had come to the point of acceptance, assuring their sons and daughters that they were still loved. Two of the students in her group, on the other hand, had been virtually disowned. One other friend had yet to tell his parents he was gay, even though on campus he'd been out for more than a year.

Eventually, Valerie went to the counseling center and found a therapist she liked. Together they began preparing for the day she would offer the truth to her parents.

When it comes to adjusting to new settings, there may be lessons to learn from families who have already developed some important relocation skills before their sons or daughters are ready to matriculate.

One technique—"quick nesting"—is used by many families that frequently relocate due to the occupational requirements of one or both parents—be it in the military, in other forms of government service, or in the private sector. Such families tend to focus on two basic relocation requirements: re-creating some semblance of familiarity wherever they go and putting in place the basic support services they need as quickly as possible.

Jean and Jerry Wright live in Ottawa, Ontario. They have three adult children: Nick, who graduated from London University; Terry, a senior at University of British Colombia in Vancouver; and Kelly, a freshman at Trinity College in Dublin, Ireland. It may sound exotic, but the Wrights are a "regular" family from whom some important lessons can be derived.

The Wrights lived overseas most of their kids' lives. They spent many years in the Philippines and a few in Bangladesh. While these experiences tended to lessen the anxiety the Wright parents felt concerning the college transition for their kids, what is interesting is that they were careful not to take for granted the adaptive skills these young people possessed.

"We found it important to be with them the first few days (upon arriving at school)," said Jean. "It helped the kids feel secure to have us there and making sure that everything was as it should be: school fees paid, making sure that expected housing was available and acceptable, and setting up bank accounts, phone connections, and computer access."

In the beginning of each child's school year, both Jean and Jerry called their fledgling to see how they were doing, before the student called them. They wanted to be sure that their sons and daughter did not feel alone and that they were aware that someone wanted to know how they were doing. That support is important, said Jean, when they are asking themselves the question, "Can I deal with life in the big, wide world?"

Surprisingly, even with all of their overseas living experiences, an important source of advice for these parents turned out to be the summer camp brochures they had received in earlier years—the ones that recommended that parents write letters, but not tell the son or daughter how much they were missed. "Don't make them feel guilty for leaving you," Jean said. She went on to express her concern that a lot of parents seem to put emotional baggage on their child about leaving. "You might be at home crying your eyes out because you miss them, but don't tell them that," she said.

College counselors echo the same idea—there is an important balance between letting the student know you care and are available, yet avoiding the temptation to burden him with your own separation pangs.

While Jean and Jerry's family may be unique in some ways, the telling point in their story is the importance of helping students get settled in before leaving them to take on classes, a new social life, and all the other aspects of college.

Parental role: Support in, control out

Helping your student get settled in leaves her comfortable and assured, but college is the time for your student to take responsibility and solve her own problems. When your teenager becomes a college student, it is time to be supportive, not controlling.

A university faculty member explained that students who are majoring in one of the social service programs in the Applied Human Services Department are required to meet with their academic advisor for a comprehensive advising session. The purpose of the session is to ensure that students are fully aware of all program requirements, have examined all of the various options available within the program as well as in related programs, and have a clear idea of the career potentials they will encounter if they complete their degree in that area. The meeting is for students and academic advisors only; parents are asked not to attend.

One mother was particularly unhappy about this policy. She accompanied her daughter to the appointment and repeatedly asked to attend the session, while her daughter became visibly uncomfortable. Finally, the mother asked where the session would be conducted, waited until the student entered the room with the advisor, and then proceeded to exit the building and position herself under the window of the meeting room in an attempt to listen in on the conversation.

As we have been saying all along, it is the student who must learn to adjust and take responsibility. The "helicopter" mother in this story was clearly over the line, unable to allow her daughter to interpret information, ask relevant questions, or even relate the conversation to her mother afterward.

Dr. Robert Portnoy with the University of Nebraska tells parents that "maintaining a supportive relationship with your children can be critical to their success in college, particularly during their first year." He says that even if your relationship with your student was strained or distant during high school, it is still important to convey your support once your child leaves home. Sometimes the space and distance allowed by a move to campus is just what the parent/child relationship needs. While Portnoy encourages parents to maintain regular contact with their student, he also advises that they give the student space to initiate phone calls and conversations. "Respect and support his or her right to make independent decisions," Portnoy says, while letting them know "you will serve as an advocate and an advisor when asked." Don't be hurt, though, if your student asks for help one day, then rejects you the next; it is all part of the process. Students need support and encouragement while they explore and adapt to their new situation, but they need to do so without Mom or Dad looking over their shoulder. They need to feel connected, but also free to make their own choices. Once again, the issue is finding the correct balance, and it is best if that balance is found when your teenager is still at home.

By the last couple of years of high school, Derek was making most of his own decisions about school, activities, and life in general. He knew his parents trusted him, and Derek respected their expectations. He didn't have a curfew because he came in at reasonable hours and always let his parents know what was going on; communication between them was open and productive. When he was accepted at an out-of-state school, Derek said he wasn't overwhelmed with "tons of new freedoms" because he hadn't been severely restricted by overprotective parents during high school.

"I'm successful using my own resources," Derek says. "I'm comfortable talking with my professors," something he thinks many college students avoid because they just don't know how to talk with adults. "It's a shame," Derek says. "The professor is their most valuable tool."

Derek credits his ability to develop relationships with adults to the fact that his parents always volunteered in the activities in which he chose to participate, such as sports and Boy Scouts. "My parents showed me that I could have relationships with adults."

Although Derek is doing well on his own at school and is an upperclassman, he still remains in close contact with his parents. Their support is important, whether it comes in the form of listening to problems, relaying the latest news from home, or mailing a package of chocolates. As Derek and all students advance through the changes and adjustments of their years at school, parents need to listen and support. It is often during the later years that difficult academic choices have to be made, lifestyle changes may occur, friendships or romances end. It is in the later years that the student is most likely to be living off campus, where the tripling up of roommates and more unrestrained partying may occur, and where a non-rent-paying roommate can have drastic consequences for the others who share the apartment or rental house.

While students are going through all these changes they need to feel connected. This was one of the most commonly stated and emphasized themes in interviews with campus counselors. The counselor's focus is in facilitating the transition process, helping students avoid problems of isolation or unhealthy relationships, making certain students are accessing the services they need. All of this, however, is considerably influenced by the nature of the relationship between students and their parents.

Sometimes tensions arise when a student seeks professional counseling while at school. Parents can sometimes feel threatened by this idea, wondering why their guidance and support weren't sufficient, wondering what the student is telling the counselor about the family, or worried that something is happening that their son or daughter is hiding. At that point, it is important for parents to remember two things: first, counseling is not intended or designed as a replacement for parenting, and second, everyone needs feedback from outside the family from time to time, and that feedback needs to be responsibly given.

Since some students arrive on campus having previously experienced therapy or counseling, they may be more predisposed to seek help than students without those earlier experiences. If, on the other hand, the previous experience was not successful or was in some sense unpleasant, they may have to be reminded that counseling relationships can vary, and they may need to look for a counselor with whom they feel more comfortable. In any case, the parent can provide some useful support by making certain the student knows what kind of services are available and where to find them. Once again, remember the importance of orientation programs as well as Web site information.

It is also important to remember, as noted in previous chapters, that privacy laws enter into this picture as well as the traditional confidentiality of the counselor-client relationship. Counselors reported n interviews that parents often call to inquire how their student is doing, and this is understandable since the student clearly has some issues he s dealing with—the reason he is in counseling in the first place. What is sometimes difficult, however, is for parents to accept the idea that the only information they can be given concerning what goes on in counseling is from the student himself.

However, as counselors have pointed out, it is sometimes helpful to the parent to just call up the counselor and talk about their own anxieties. After all, it is the family that is making the transition, not just the student. While counselors can't reveal the content of a student's counseling sessions, they can often provide reassurance to the parents concerning the student's situation.

Bolstering emotional strength

Knowing that you will need to "let go" of your fledgling college student at the right time is one thing, but how can you prepare both yourself and your teenager in advance? According to Jody Donovan of Colorado State, the best preparation is simply discussing with your student the range of feelings you mostly likely will experience. Be honest about feeling sad that he is moving away from home, but emphasize the excitement you feel for his new beginnings. Create opportunities for your teenager to experience time away from home. Be it summer camp, two weeks with Aunt Sue and Uncle Bill, or a summer college study program, Joyce Caufman, an educational consultant and former high school counselor, recommends giving your teenager the opportunity, and responsibility, to be on his own.

When her sons were ages four and two, Patti and her husband, Carl, moved to a developing country for Carl's work. Each summer for six years, Patti and her young sons would fly home for a visit; Carl would come a few weeks later. Even though flying halfway around the world with young children was a challenge, Patti noted that her boys quickly became seasoned veterans. "Shortly after takeoff, they would ask the stewardess for headphones, a deck of cards, and a Coke," Patti said. "Then they'd settle in for the long flights."

Once back living in the United States, as each boy reached the age of sixteen, they were given the opportunity to return to foreign lands during one of their father's business trips. When her older son Geoff's turn came, Patti was quite nervous because Geoff was going to be traveling by himself to meet up with his father. "He had three stopovers and that included a night over in Bangkok," Patti remembered. "He had to leave the airport, get to a hotel, and return the next day for his flight. I kept checking the airline Web site to see where his flights were the whole way." Patti said that she calculated the time difference and called the hotel in Bangkok an hour before Geoff needed to leave for the airport for his final leg of the journey, but he was up and ready to go. Patti was finally relieved when she received word he had met up with his father. Patti went through the same anxieties when her younger son, Nick, turned sixteen and made a similar journey.

Patti is quick to say that both boys had a great sixteenth-year experience that gave them confidence in their abilities to take care of themselves. Geoff has carried that experience with him to college, where he has been successful in his studies and living arrangements. Patti has no doubt that Nick, who is contemplating college for next year, also will adjust well to being on his own. In the meantime, both boys took time off and are gaining even more independence experience as, together, they travel and work in Peru. Patti believes that although her sons still make "questionable" decisions, they are quite capable of taking care of themselves whether it be in college or life beyond.

Remember back to your children's days in elementary school and the expectations you made known to your child. Did you stress that she does her best academically? Did you teach him the golden rule? As your children enter the teenage years, be sure they still understand your expectations, Caufman says. If you have built expectations into their teenage years, they will carry those into college; don't wait to have one big lecture right before they leave home. Caufman told of one family that expected a certain grade point average from their students. If the student stayed above the average, the parents would pay for all the college expenses; if he or she fell below, the student assumed the responsibility of all college costs. "Of their three children, only one fell below the average and it was only for one semester," Caufman said. The same goes for expectations regarding behavior. Drinking, drugs, sexual behaviors, and healthy choices need to be discussed throughout the high school years.

Another opportunity is to introduce your high school student to college students who are willing to discuss the transition process. Listening to a peer who is currently immersed in the college scene, and succeeding, is a powerful catalyst for the uncertain teenager.

Preparing Your Teenager: Grow Their Independence

Your teenager is going through many changes and will soon be leaving home. It is important to provide him with opportunities to rely on himself, to cope with new or uncomfortable situations, and to develop his own opinions. Such skills will help him adjust to college and life beyond high school.

1) Encourage opportunities for your teenager to "branch out" without family.

Challenge	Solution
In his freshman year, your teenager comes home excited about a European spring break travel opportunity that a teacher at his school is organizing. The thought of him going so far away without family is a bit frightening.	Many schools offer school-sponsored travel—wonderful opportunities for teenagers to branch out without family. The first thing to consider is cost. Is a fund-raising project available? If not, is there another way your teenager can earn at least part of the money? Insisting on his earning all or part of the cost lets him "own" the trip. If you are uncomfortable with the idea, ask for information from the teacher. The teacher will have strict conduct and behavior rules for the participants, as well as an organized plan. If the money issue can be solved, such school trips offer a great "on his own" experience.
Every other summer, your family travels to Canada to visit good friends who have children the same age as yours. It is time again to go, but a conflict will keep your family from traveling. The Canadians, however, suggest you send your teenager for a visit on her own. Your daughter, who has never traveled alone, is all for it.	Again, this is a great opportunity for your teenager to branch out without family. She will be with good friends with whom you are completely comfortable. Most likely, you can find a nonstop flight, but if not, making a plane change is not too difficult and gives her a low-risk responsibility. Your friends are bound to give you a full report on her behavior, she will recognize your trust, and she will gain confidence in her ability to go it alone.

Challenge	Solution
Your church youth group is planning a mission trip to Mexico and your teenager wants to go. It is an inexpensive trip, but you are worried about safety issues.	Although safety is always an issue in travel, most school, church, or other such organizations offer trips that have been researched for safety issues, and trips are cancelled if concerns warrant. In this situation, your teenager will be with a trusted group doing meaningful work. Even though it is inexpensive, again consider having your teenager earn the money. This is another good opportunity for him to branch out.

2) Help your teenager adjust to new or uncomfortable situations.

Challenge	Solution
Due to a change in employment, your family moves to another part of the country before your teenager's sophomore year. Your teenager is upset and angry at you for moving her away from her friends. She comes home in tears from her new school, saying she hates it and has no friends.	Although you know that she will eventually make friends, do not deride her concerns. Confirm that her feelings are legitimate, but also try to focus on things that interest her. What organizations, clubs, or sports is she interested in? Help her research what her school offers and encourage her to get involved. Follow up daily by asking how things are going. Most likely she will make a friend or two within a short period of time. Encourage her to invite a new friend over for pizza and a movie, and let things take off from there. Revisit the issue in a few months, complementing her on her ability to adapt and get involved.

Challenge	Solution
Last summer your teenager and his best friend went to a weeklong summer camp for soccer players. They enjoyed it and you put a deposit down for him to go again. A couple of days before the camp begins, your son's friend pulls out because of a family emergency. Now your son claims he won't go; at this late date the camp will not refund your money.	Let your teenager know that you are sorry about his friend, but remind him that he is committed to go with or without the friend. Remind him of how much he enjoyed it last summer and that most likely some of the kids he met last year will attend again. Explain that you cannot get a refund and that it is important to fulfill commitments even when circumstances change. When he returns—hopefully after having another positive experience—praise him for making the most of it, and point out how well he handled things.
A relative who runs a farm in a rural area calls and offers your teenager a summer job. Your son enjoyed the farm as a boy, but now he says he doesn't want to go because it would be boring.	Although you should not force your teenager to take the job, it is a great opportunity. Ask him what plans he has for the summer. Hopefully, you already have made it clear that you expect him to do something constructive during the summer, whether a job, working at home, or volunteer work. Point out how difficult it is for teenagers to find jobs, and explain how important working experience will be to him. Together, figure out how much money he could make at the farm—that should be an incentive. Be willing to compromise—maybe he could work half of the summer or break it up in segments that allow him to spend some time with friends. However it works out, it will provide him with good experience, increase his confidence, and provide him with his own money.

) Keep communication open despite your teenager's changing views.

Challenge	Solution
Your family has always been active in your religious community. Now that your daughter is in high school, she claims she no longer believes and says you cannot force her to participate.	This can be an emotional issue for many families, but it is a common scenario. You ultimately have the final say, but consider seeking advice from your religious leaders or parents who have gone through a similar situation. What is the result of forcing the teenager to participate? Can you reach a compromise? Ask your teenager to explain her beliefs and truly listen. Explain to her why participation is important to you. Consider a compromise of her participating part of the time, and ask her to keep you informed of the development of her new beliefs. Show her that your beliefs are important, but that you love her despite her changing views.
You consider yourself moderately involved in current events, but politics usually do not come up in family conversation. Your teenager takes a required government class and suddenly becomes passionate about politics. He expresses his views often and you are not comfortable with his ideas. Sometimes you argue with him even though neither one of you have all the facts.	Remember that it is normal for teenagers to sometimes reject the viewpoints of their parents. Your teenager has discovered a subject in which he is passionately interested. Encourage him to research all sides of the issue—even doing so yourself and giving him Web links or articles to read. Have set rules for discussions, so that opposing ideas do not result in arguments—modeling how to handle conflicts. Show him that his changing views will not change your love for him.

4) Make your expectations clear.

Challenge	Solution
Now that your teenager has started high school, you expect her to be serious about her studies. You know that her grades will be considered when she applies to college, and you assume she knows how important that is. At parent-teacher conferences, however, you discover she has one B, three Cs, and two Ds.	Do not assume that your expectations are the same as your teenager's. Call a meeting and tell her what you expect academically and behaviorally, and why. Explain that her efforts in school reflect her work ethic and dedication to the task at hand. If she wants to go to college, have her research a college of her choice and find out what are the academic requirements for acceptance. This also is a good time to explain your expectations for college. If you will be paying her tuition and fees, what are you expecting her to achieve? If she falls short, what are the consequences?
You consider your teenager a confident, fairly responsible young man. He is making good grades in school, and he tells you he wants to apply for a part-time job. You expect that he will do just fine with another responsibility. He lands a job at a local restaurant working three nights a week. Before long, his grades start slipping, he is not available for chores at home, and he misses many family activities.	Once again, make your expectations clear. Tell him that when you approved his taking a job, that you expected him to put school first and keep up his grades. You also expect him to do a certain number of chores around the house and participate in family activities. Making his own money is probably important to him, so try to reach a compromise. Suggest he cut back on his hours or change his working schedule so it does not conflict with heavy homework nights. Together make a compromised list of chores and family expectations. Give him time to try out the new schedule, but set a time to re-evaluate. Keep your expectations clear, but be open to his ideas.

Chapter Eight

The transition from dependency on parents to relying on themselves is a big and important step for teenagers. Encourage and guide your teenager, and provide opportunities for her to move beyond the familiarity of home to discover just what she is capable of accomplishing. Such revelations tend to build confidence and capability, resulting in teenagers who are ready to successfully transition to college.

Chapter 9

Finances 101:
Figuring and Managing Money

One thing you certainly knew before picking up this book: College is expensive. According to the College Board's 2008–09 statistics, the average cost of attending a four-year public university, including housing and fees, is $15,213 per year, a 5.9 percent increase over the previous school year. Out-of-state costs for the same institution were $26,741, a 6 percent increase. The average cost of a private, not-for-profit, four-year college was $35,636, a 4.3 percent increase over the previous year. Even though those figures are the published costs of attending college and do not reflect grants, scholarships, or financial aid, the cost of higher education is daunting. Despite the fact that most Americans don't have thousands of dollars just lying around and the fact that the average public college student graduates with a debt of $15,500 while their average private college counterpart graduates with a debt of $19,500, most parents believe that a college education is either necessary or at least helpful for their student's life successes. The College Board adds credence to those beliefs in its 2009 report on Trends in Higher Education by stating: "Median income for families with a householder with at least a four-year college degree is more than $50,000 per year higher than for those with only a high school education." Short of winning the lottery or robbing a bank, how can parents and students afford such an endeavor? Moreover, who pays for what? Do Mom and Dad, or Josh or Sarah define the costs, and, most importantly, do Josh and Sarah know how to manage their money?

Who pays for what?

Parents and students often have different ideas on who should be responsible for the various costs involved with going to college. The expectations should be clear before the start of classes.

Jon chose Colorado State University because it was close to home and he would be paying in-state tuition. His parents agreed to help him with the cost of books, but basically Jon was on his own. He was responsible for tuition, fees, parking costs, upkeep and insurance on his car, and gas. He chose to live at home and commute to save money on housing and food. For his first year, Jon said he had $3,000 in student loans. "Next year I will claim myself independent of my parents on my tax form," Jon said. "That will make me eligible for more scholarships and grants. And I intend to move out of my parent's house. I am going to be renting a room at the Baptist Student Union apartments for $300 a month."

Many students, like Jon, struggle to find ways to finance their education, while others have substantial help from parents. Although that help is usually given in good faith, it is important that parents and students are clear about what that help is for. Tuition, fees, books, room, and board seem to be the obvious categories, but beyond that, basics and frills can easily become blurred depending on whether it is Mom and Dad or Sarah and Josh talking. Does Josh need a car at school? How much is parking? What is the bus system like on and off campus? What about a bicycle? Does a long board count as transportation? How does Sarah get home for holidays and visits?

While those questions pertain to transportation, the list goes on. Parents and students need to discuss cell phones, Internet fees, laundry costs, medical expenses, eating out, and the endless issue of entertainment possibilities, including spring break getaways. College students need ime off also, but concerts, beach trips, and ski days take a dip out of omebody's earnings, and it is a much smoother encounter if the payee las been determined long before an activity begins. Parents need to clearly tate what they are willing to pay for before Josh is tucked away in his lorm room, so that he can begin working summers or weekends during ligh school to put away his own college expense money.

It was the end of February of Brian's freshman year when his mom got the call that so many parents get from their college student. "Mom, I'm almost out of money," Brian started. "Oh," Kathleen said. "You had $2,000 from your summer job. Is it really all gone?"

"Well, most of it went to the ski trip to Jackson Hole over Christmas break," Brian continued.

"We gave you some toward that trip as a Christmas present," his mother pointed out, but Brian admitted the trip turned out to cost more than he expected.

"I was wondering if you and Dad would consider giving me a loan until the summer, when I can get another job and pay you back."

Kathleen told Brian that she and his dad could help him, but Brian would have to provide them with a budget and a list of expenses he would need covered through the end of the year before they could agree on how much. Brian said he would work on those requests, but a couple of days later he called back, much more upbeat.

"Hey, Mom, forget the loan," Brian said. "I just got a job with the on-campus catering service. I sign up on a weekly basis to work a banquet—I can work around my school schedule and they said I would make about $60 a banquet." Brian ended up working two or three banquets a week and didn't need the loan from his parents. Most important, Kathleen said, he learned how one activity could take a huge chunk of his savings.

Brian figured out a solution based on conversations he had with his parents before he went to college. He knew he would be responsible for extras such as ski passes, concert tickets, and new video games. He solved his problem by securing an on-campus job that easily worked around his schedule and gave him the pocket money he felt he needed to survive to the end of the semester. Holding a job while in college may sound like the obvious answer, but working presents time challenges that some students cannot handle. It is easy to get overwhelmed with work while taking a full load of classes, and students and parents should carefully consider limits. The usual expectation, as conveyed at many orientation sessions, is that students should spend two to three hours studying and preparing for every hour they spend in class. If that student is also working thirty hours a week, something has to give. Administrators say that, unfortunately, it is usually schoolwork that gives.

"Money really stresses out kids," noted Sakura, an education major at Montana State University. She advises students to save as much as they can before coming to college so that they are not forced to work all the time. Sakura observed that many students have to pay for everything: tuition, books, room and board, car expenses. Those students, she said, end up working forty hours a week somewhere off-campus while taking at least twelve hours of class. "Those are the people that when you ask them how they are doing, they roll their eyes and say they are too busy," she said. "You want them to say, 'just fine,' but work and school is more than they can handle."

Jill Kreutzer, retired from Colorado State University's Department of Human Development and Family Studies agrees with Sakura. She advises that students do not work their first semester at school; instead they should concentrate on succeeding in school and in their new living situation. After that they should restrict working to fifteen to twenty hours per work, preferably with an on-campus job that will flex with their schedule. Too often, she said, overworked students drop difficult courses or change to an "easier" major because they cannot manage working and going to school.

Amy was a manager at Sonic Drive In. She made good tips, enjoyed her job, and did not want to go to college, but she felt pressured by her parents to go to school and be successful in her studies like her older sister. During her freshman year, Amy barely passed her classes. She changed majors four times, trying to find an "easier" major. Her priority was work and hanging out with her friends, and, consequently, her grades were low and she was placed on academic probation. Despite probation, Amy continued to focus on work. She ended up with an academic suspension and was unable to return to school for two years.

Kreutzer said that college students need to ease into working and that school should always come first. She pointed out that students feel so much pressure to make money that they give their job priority over their schoolwork. "A mediocre job should not come first," Kreutzer said. "The job needs to flex for school and the student."

With an average middle-class income, Carole and Don paid for almost everything involving their three children's college educations. Even in the summers, they did not pressure their kids to work long hours. Their youngest worked summers at a local Boy Scout Camp where she did not make much money but had experiences that Carole and Don felt were important. "We want our kids to have lots of experiences, so we are willing to pay more (for college expenses) if it means they don't get high-paying jobs during the summers or during the school year," Carole explained. For Carole and Don's children, those experiences have included semesters abroad and humanitarian work in Central America. Two of the couple's three well-adjusted kids have graduated and hold paying jobs, while the youngest is currently volunteering in an orphanage in Nepal before returning to finish her final year of school.

Payment options

As you and your student discuss expenses, financial responsibilities, and working, the big issue will undoubtedly be threading its way through your college planning process: Where is the money going to come from? There are hundreds of sources to consult on the issue of financing a college education, and this book does not attempt to cover them all. Instead, the hope is to direct parents to the more common routes and encourage families to thoroughly research their options in advance of their student's senior year of high school. Obviously, the sooner parents begin planning financially for their children's education, the less financial stress is encountered.

Saving

Back when Sarah and Josh were born, Grandma and Grandpa took out a college savings account, Certificate of Deposit, or some other savings depository. Over the years, Christmas and birthday checks were deposited, but probably not much accrued. Now Sarah and Josh are juniors in high school, there are still fifteen years left on their parents' mortgage, brother Will needs braces, Grandma needs to be moved into an assisted living facility, the roof needs replacing, there are rumors that layoffs are coming at work, and college is looming. It feels like that $4,000 in the college savings account might as well be $40.

Of course, $4,000 won't last long, but never discourage such meager beginnings toward your child's college education. If securing a college education for your child is important, make a definite plan to start saving. Talk to a financial advisor about the best way to save, then do it.

Delores, a single parent since her three children were preschoolers, started saving for their college education when they were in elementary school. Living in Dallas, Delores explained that she opened an account for each child in the Texas Tomorrow Fund, a college savings plan that was a predecessor to and works similarly to 529 accounts. Her oldest is now a student at the University of Arkansas, and Delores was happy to learn that she could use the Texas Tomorrow Fund to pay for her daughter's education expenses. As a bonus, because her daughter received high SAT scores, the University of Arkansas granted her in-state tuition.

Parents should consider multiple options when tucking money away for their child's education. One increasingly popular choice, which Delores mentioned, is the use of 529 plans—a college education investment account that allows you to save and then use the money for education expenses tax-free. The plans are administered by each state, so you need to check on the specifics of the state in which you reside, but the fund can be used for any college or university. Another option is an educational IRA, which was renamed in 2002 as Coverdell Education Savings Account. These accounts work similarly to IRAs in that there is a maximum amount you can contribute each year and the accounts are tax-free under most circumstances. Uniform Gift/Transfers to Minors Accounts are another option that allows savings to be set up in the name of a child (under age eighteen to twenty-one, depending on the state), but names an adult as custodian of the account until the child comes of age. These accounts are taxed at 10 percent, usually a tax break for the adult in charge. Be warned, however, that when the child comes of age and becomes custodian of the account, he may not use it for books and college fees as you had imagined. Instead, your son might decide it is a great way to get that car he dreamed of for so long. Another option is simply an earmarked taxable investment account. Under each of these options, parents should understand fully the way the plan works before making a decision.

Freebies

While saving is the best way to prepare for college costs, applying for scholarships and grants is a smart move for anyone considering higher education.

Rosie knew that she would need scholarships and other financial aid to pay for her college education. She had a big jump on the process by graduating in the top 3 percent of her high school class, so she was an attractive college candidate. First, however, Rosie did a college search online, looking particularly in the Northwest, an area that interested her. She toured some college campuses with her father and decided on Southern Oregon University, a college nestled in a beautiful setting that offered small classes and exciting outdoor opportunities. Once accepted, Rosie focused on scholarships offered by the school and federal grants. She received both based on academics and need. She also participated in work-study on campus as a receptionist at the school's art museum, which earned her $2,000 a year. Despite the scholarships and grants, Rosie still needed to take out a small loan to cover all her expenses. The loan, Rosie said, is small enough for her to handle, she likes her new school, and she is off to a great start.

We all know it is a great idea to save for the future, but the reality is that it often does not happen. Regardless of whether there is a savings account waiting to be tapped, every college-bound student should actively explore scholarships and grants as Rosie did. No matter if it is a few hundred dollars or a full-ride scholarship, it is worth the effort to apply. Take note: It will be an effort. There are thousands of scholarships offered every year and looking for the right ones can be overwhelming.

High school counselors, of course, offer scholarship guidance, but remember that they are helping more than just your student and they cannot possibly be aware of all the best matches for your son or daughter.

The counselor may suggest certain scholarship Web sites for your student to explore, including www.fastweb.com, one of the best-known scholarship search sites. Note that Fastweb is a free Web site; never pay to find scholarships—the information is out there and free. Fastweb requires students to answer several questions about themselves before offering the best possible scholarship matches. This effort toward self-awareness is an important step in the matching process, explained Joyce Caufman, a Colorado-based educational consultant and retired high school counselor. Caufman starts her clients with a self-awareness exploration to determine who they are and what they want. "The self-awareness piece is critical," Caufman said. If a scholarship is determined by an essay or interview, the student must be able to articulate who they are and how they fit the scholarship requirements.

Maddie was certain she would major in art in college. But to be sure, she participated in a self-awareness questionnaire and, surprising to Maddie, found herself pointed in another direction. All the tests indicated that Maddie's real talent was helping other people. As Maddie thought about it, it began to make sense. She was usually moved to action by the unfortunate situations of others, as she was by the Katrina hurricane disaster in 2005. Frustrated by what she saw on television, Maddie organized a fund-raiser and raised $3,600 in one weekend for Katrina victims. With help from a counselor, Maddie explored careers in which she could combine art and assisting people in need, for example, art therapy or producing marketing materials for a nonprofit. Excited by the prospects, Maddie applied to colleges and for scholarships with a better focus.

Caufman related another idea Maddie should consider when applying for scholarships and schools: look for schools that are building up the department in which the student is interested. In Maddie's case, she would look at schools that are building their art or social science departments. Those schools are more likely to offer scholarships to students interested in their burgeoning departments, but there are many other factors to consider when searching for scholarships, Caufman said. Be aware that students who academically make the top 25 percent of their high school class are more likely to get scholarships, whether they have the financial need or not—you were right, those high school grades are important. Search for scholarships that match your student's major, activities, and location, and even check if the school offers scholarships for siblings. Don't forget that there are some odd scholarships available, such as the one offered by Duck Tape: high school students all over the country compete for the scholarship by making their prom clothes out of Duck Tape. Another important source is that of local community scholarships. Most high schools will offer information about local scholarships, but it is up to the student to apply, so be on the lookout for information from the school about the application deadline. And while your high school senior is applying for scholarships, consider that there are many scholarships available for upperclassmen who have proven their ability to succeed in college. So while high school senior Josh is filling out applications, his older college sophomore sister should be filling out her own applications to help her through her last couple of years.

One last thing to remember when searching for scholarships: private colleges and universities with large endowments usually have more monetary incentive to offer students than public institutions. While the overall cost of tuition and fees are much higher in private institutions, their scholarship offers can make the cost comparable, or even cheaper, than state institutions. Dust off your calculator and start the figuring. You and your student may be surprised at how the numbers point you toward universities and colleges that may have seemed out of financial reach.

During a high school thespians conference, Elise was approached by representatives from the University of Evansville. The school offered a strong drama program and they urged her to apply. Elise's high GPA and test scores made her quite attractive to the university, and they offered her a $12,000 annual

Performing Arts Scholarship. Once in school, Elise discovered she could earn an additional $500 per year for high grades.

When Elise's sister applied to Evansville, they granted her an $11,000 annual academic scholarship, with a bonus of $1,500 because she was a sibling of a current Evansville student. The scholarships, plus a low-interest, private loan that their mother found, has made the private school quite affordable for the sisters.

Loans

Even if Josh and Sarah are busy writing essays for scholarship applications, unless that 529 account is chock-full of money, there is a good chance they will need to apply for a loan. According to the College Board's 2009 Trends in Student Aid, in school year 2008¬09, 42 percent of public institution students and 55 percent of private, not-for-profit institution students took on federal student loans to fund their education. An additional 15 percent of all undergraduate students took on non-federal loans to fund their education. Those figures do not include credit card debt to help finance education, but according to Sallie Mae's Undergraduate Student and Credit Cards 2009 report, nine of every ten undergraduate credit card holders pay for direct college expenses with their credit cards (see Last resort: Credit cards).

The first loan-research step is the federally funded loan. You should make it mandatory that your student complete the FAFSA (Free Application for Federal Student Aid). High schools always provide information about FAFSA, including how and when to apply. With that lengthy application, the government will estimate your student's eligibility for the various types of federal student loans and grants. We will not attempt to explain all the loans available from the government, but you and your student should make sure you understand all the terms for the loans and/or grants for which your student is eligible. Be aware that while federal loans defer payments while the student is still in school, the loans continue to build on top of each other, leaving some students to face large amounts of debt upon graduation.

If for some reason your child is not eligible for federal loans, or your family does not qualify for the amount you need, there are plenty of private loaning institutions ready and waiting. In fact, if you have a senior in high school or a college student, you and they probably have been bombarded with loaning advertisement through the mail. Again, this book cannot advise you on which loans to consider, only advise you to proceed with caution as you would toward any loan. Of course, even if a student believes she is proceeding with caution, the outcome is not always satisfactory, as the following story illustrates.

Rebecca understood from the beginning that she would be dependent on loans for her college education. Her parents did not have the money to finance her path to becoming an architect. Although they signed for the federal Parent Plus Loan, Rebecca accepted the responsibility for paying off the loan once she finished school. As an undergraduate at the University of Indiana, Rebecca said she occasionally took out small private loans to help defray her living expenses and other related college costs. Although she always held a part-time job, she was constantly short of money.

"I began receiving notices that some of my private loans were sold to different entities," Rebecca explained. "That was always okay with me as long as the payment continued to be deferred until I graduated." Some of her loans changed hands as many as three times, but when she was ready to start graduate school, she was contacted by some of the institutions to begin payment. Rebecca figures she missed certain details about deferment during the shuffling of her loans. She was faced with starting graduate school, out-of-state tuition for a program at Virginia Tech, and paying off some of her loans. Rebecca turned again to loaning institutes, continuing the cycle of obtaining loans to pay off previous loans.

Rebecca graduated with $150,000 of undergraduate and graduate loan debt. She is now working at an architectural firm in San Francisco and is in the process yet again, of consolidating her loans, this time she hopes for the last time.

"It is really depressing," Rebecca said. "I have my first job, but I'm so much in debt that it keeps me from getting excited about life." To save money, Rebecca shares a bedroom with a friend, uses public transportation, and takes advantage of San Francisco's free activities, but she still pays $700 a month in rent (quite reasonable for San Francisco) and her monthly loan payments equal $1,000. Her salary is $2,600 per month.

"Honestly, I don't know what I could have done differently," Rebecca says looking back at those years of racking up college debt. "I had good grades, I worked as much as I could, and I had no family help. I was on my own, trying to find a balance on how I lived and what I had to do to get by."

As Rebecca's story shows, student loans can easily grow out of control. According to the College Board's 2009 Trends in Student Aid, "among 2007–08 bachelor's degree recipients, 34 percent graduated with no education debt, but 10 percent had borrowed $40,000 or more." The situation can become worse with credit card use.

Last resort: Credit cards

How many credit card applications do you get in the mail each month? Most of us have probably lost count. According to a testimony by Harvard Law School Professors Elizabeth Warren and Leo Gottlieb before the Senate Committee on Banking, Housing, and Urban Affairs in January 2007, more than six billion preapproved credit card solicitations were mailed in the United States in 2006. That included extensive advertising and direct marketing on college campuses. Most of us would agree with Warren and Gottlieb that credit card agreements are incomprehensible—

and who reads page after page of that tiny print? The two professors contend that virtually all credit card companies will impose extravagant fees and penalties for missed or late payments, sucking people further and further into debt. If we grown-up, middle-age adults fall prey to the seemingly unbreakable cycle of credit card debt, how do we expect our fledging eighteen- or nineteen-year-old who is offered a free lunch outside the student center for just filling out the application, to say no?

Elise saw the flyers around the University of Evansville campus as she went to and from classes. Elise said the flyer immediately caught her attention: "Free Pizza." She noticed, however, that the fine print requested that students bring their school ID and a driver's license.

The pizza joint was crowded with hungry students, and there was a long line to reach the free pizza. "They told us that to get the pizza, we first had to fill out a form that asked for our name, address, social security number, and even our mother's maiden name," Elise said. "I was suspicious, so I made up a social security number and gave a fake maiden name for my mom. Then they checked our ID to make sure we hadn't lied about our name and address."

Within a few weeks, Elise received a couple of approved credit cards at her parents' home in Colorado, despite the fake social security number. Elise opted to tear them up, she said, as all she wanted was free pizza. "They never made it clear that the form was a credit card application," Elise said. "There were so many kids around, all wanting pizza, that the purpose seemed secondary."

Elise tore up the unwanted credit cards, but many students will accept them eagerly. When they do take the responsibility of using a credit card, they had better understand what pitfalls await them, say financial experts, counselors, and parents who have avoided credit card traps. Train your children early in basic money management, make sure they fully understand how credit cards make money, go over a credit card bill with them, advise them on the best time to obtain a credit card and what to use it for, and train them to pay the balance, in full, every month. Don't forget to train them to carefully read their credit card bill each month and question any suspicious charges.

Excitement abounded when Shannon and some of her fellow architecture students decided to study abroad in Italy. It was an expensive endeavor, however, and some students had to drop the idea because of the cost. Shannon knew that Jamie, one of her closest friends and a roommate, would have difficulty paying for it. Jamie told Shannon that her father had recently been laid off, but even after Shannon overheard Jamie's "heated, screaming matches" with her parents over the issue, Jamie still signed up to go.

The experience in Italy was as wonderful as Shannon had hoped. After the study was over, Shannon and some other students extended their stay in Europe to travel and sightsee. Jamie, out of funds, flew home. While in London, Shannon's mom called to ask her about a $400 charge on the American Express card that Shannon was carrying for emergencies. Shannon honestly told her mother she had never used the card the entire trip. After disputing the charge, the credit card company traced the charge to Jamie's college account—the account she used to pay tuition. Shannon, checking the date of the charge, recalled that she had been out late that evening in Italy but had left her wallet in the studio where she worked alongside Jamie and other students. She was dumbfounded at the idea that Jamie had stolen from her, and she alerted her other friends about the situation.

Sure enough, over a month later, another of Shannon's friends who had studied in Italy discovered a suspicious charge on her credit card account, charged on the same day for the same amount. A couple of weeks later, another friend found the same on her account. It seemed as if Jamie had tried to divide the charges to a small enough amount on each card so that her friends wouldn't notice. Shannon's mother did notice and Shannon's friends learned the importance of checking their credit card accounts.

Obviously, Jamie's story is one of theft, but it is important to note that most of the students she was with had credit cards. Sallie Mae's 2009 report on "How Undergraduate Students Use Credit Cards" states that 84 percent of undergraduates had at least one credit card, a trend that is up 76 percent since Sallie Mae completed its last study in fall 2004. The report goes on to say that 92 percent of undergraduate credit card holders charged "textbooks, school supplies, or other direct college expenses. Nearly one-third put tuition on their credit card." Credit-card-carrying freshmen carry a median debt of $939, while seniors graduate with an average debt of more than $4,100. Sallie Mae states that "one-fifth of seniors carried balances greater than $7,000." Most disconcerting is that Sallie Mae reports that 60 percent of those debt-carrying students were surprised at how high their balance was; 40 percent admitted they charged items knowing they couldn't cover the cost when the bill came due. And take note, parents: Sallie Mae reported that "one-third of students rarely or never discussed credit card use with parents. Eighty-four percent of undergraduates indicated they needed more education on financial management topics. In fact, *64 percent would have liked to receive information in high school and 40 percent as college freshman* (emphasis mine)."

Financial relationships

While your student is, hopefully, mastering the wise use of credit cards and whizzing through loan applications, keep in mind that probably for the first time in their lives they will be managing money on their own. If they live off campus, they will suddenly face managing a household with one or more roommates who may or may not consider it important to pay the electric bill on time. And what about the roommate who decides to quit paying rent at all?

Felicia, Trista, and Meredith were friends in the residence halls. As their freshman year waned, they decided to find an apartment together for the summer and the following school year. Excitedly, they signed a lease together and moved into their off-campus apartment in May. Not long after moving in, Trista started staying more often and for longer periods at her boyfriend's house. Soon she stopped paying her share of the utility bill. It wasn't long before she wrote a three-page letter to her roommates claiming that she should only pay half her share of rent because she really did not live there anymore. Alarmed, Felicia and Meredith called a house meeting and confronted Trista, who held her ground and even declared she wouldn't pay any more rent. Feeling they had no alternative, Felicia and Meredith asked Trista to move all of her things out of the apartment. The two were left with the full rent, were forced to borrow money from their parents for the remainder of the summer, and had to look for a new roommate.

Before your student signs a lease to rent an apartment or house, she should be taught to actually read the lease, question anything that is not clear, and refuse to sign if she or her roommates think part of the agreement is questionable. If you are paying for all or part of that rent, it is not unreasonable for you to read and question the lease yourself and guide your student. Even when you do so, you can be caught by surprise.

Sam and Connor moved into an apartment at the beginning of their sophomore year at the University of Colorado. The two promptly paid their bills and rent and had no financial problems. When they moved out in May, Sam's mother came to help the boys properly clean their apartment so they would receive all of their deposit money. After having scrubbed the apartment alongside the boys, Sam's mother, Eileen, was surprised when the boys received a note that said, "Clean Unit, Thanks," with a check for only 10 percent of their deposit money. Eileen called the apartment manager and found out that the apartment always charges the departing tenants the cost of a cleaning service and the cost of shampooing the carpets. There was a separate charge for cleaning window coverings, the oven, and the refrigerator. Eileen asked the manager what was the point of cleaning the unit if he was going to have a cleaning service come anyway. The manager told her that he did not charge the boys the full cost of the cleaning service because they left the unit so clean; usually the tenants left the apartments so dirty that they lost all their deposit money. Eileen argued that the window coverings were dirty when they moved in because she noted that herself, and that she personally scrubbed the refrigerator. After a bit more discussion, the apartment manager agreed to refund another 10 percent of deposit money. Remembering her own college days, Eileen said, "I always got 100 percent of my deposit back if I cleaned my apartment and left it in good shape. I had no idea that things had changed so much."

Sam and Connor may have lost a large portion of their deposit money, but they did learn to manage their household without any financial disasters. At the end of their sophomore year, they found a house to rent with two other young men, giving them another opportunity to expand their lessons in household management.

Not only do college students need to make secure arrangements with roommates for paying rent and utilities, but they also need to be careful about lending money. Jill Kreutzer, the retired Colorado State University administrator, advises students to avoid lending money to each other, period. Like many older adults, students can have a hard time saying no, particularly if a new friend asks for a few bucks to get by until the next paycheck or installment from her parents. Often, college students come with high school experiences of loaning a dollar or two to friends. Those small high school loans are often forgotten or are considered too small to cause a rift between friends. Such poor accounting can become a much bigger problem in college. The loan needed in college is more likely to be larger than a couple of bucks, and the loaner may feel the same pressure he felt in high school to help out a friend.

After his freshman year at the University of Florida, Ethan returned to his parent's home in Colorado for a summer of friends, family, and earning money as an assistant manager for Cutco Cutlery. Ethan was doing well with Cutco, earning needed money for school and expenses, and he was an advisor to other students who were starting to sell Cutco products. That summer, two start-up Cutco salesmen, both Colorado State University students, asked Ethan if he could loan them money. One of the young men asked Ethan for $140 to pay for the Cutco start-up sample kit. The other asked for $125 to help pay his rent and tide him over until he started making sales. Ethan obliged both students and the summer progressed. Ethan returned to the University of Florida in the fall, lost touch with the two students who did not continue with Cutco, and never had his loans repaid. "I didn't ask them for the money because they kept promising me they would pay me back," Ethan said. "And I could tell they were struggling financially. I've had to borrow money before and I could relate to their situation."

Ethan wishes he had that money, but it hasn't stopped him from loaning to other people. He is, however, more careful about to whom and how much he loans.

Managing a household, negotiating lease contracts, and avoiding lending are the major financial tasks awaiting the new college student. There are other money-sucking pitfalls, of course, from buying every meal out to gambling online. Again, administrators, counselors, and parents repeat their advice: Discuss money management, show your teenagers your credit card bill, have them go the grocery store and add up how much food costs there compared to driving through Taco Bell, and give them experience negotiating contracts, whether with you, their teachers, or a job.

Money management training: From age four?

It is never too early to start training your child about money—and maybe training yourself in the process. Cathy Hettleman, mother of two daughters—one in college and one in high school—and a special education teacher in Fort Collins, Colorado, has taught parenting classes for twenty years. Hettleman believes that if you do not teach children budgeting early on—from as young as age four or five—they won't get it. "I've never subscribed to the idea of giving kids money for pleasure," Hettleman said. "They need to earn it. You can match it, but they have to show some recognition of how much things cost." Hettleman advises parents to start teaching the economics of running a house from as early as age four. Teach them to save, and teach them to budget. If you decide on an allowance, tell your children they must donate a certain percentage to charity and put a certain percentage into savings. Give them a budget when you take them to the grocery store and allocate money for them to spend on vacations. "Parents don't go on vacation with an unlimited budget," Hettleman said. "Neither should the kids."

When Hettleman's daughters reached their teens, Hettleman realized their spending would go awry without strict budgeting. Although she had practiced what she preached before they reached age thirteen, she sat her girls down to compare store prices for clothing, makeup, shoes, and hair-care products. They discussed $80 name-brand jeans and $30 no-brand jeans.

Together they came up with a monthly clothing and personal care budget. Hettleman footed the bill for underwear, socks, and one pair of athletic shoes per year. For the rest, the girls had to budget. Both girls did well with their budgets, but then, they had both been budgeting from an early age. Hettleman's oldest daughter attends Chapman University in Southern California. At the costly private school, Hettleman pays for the equivalent of what it would cost her daughter to attend college at an in-state, public institution. After years of training, her daughter is very careful with her spending and always wants to be sure of who is paying for what.

Mary and Jim believed parents should buy everything for their children, instead of having the children pay a percentage from their allowance or chore wages. Their son, Brendan, grew up throwing tantrums if he was ever told no to something he wanted. He is now twenty-six years old, a graduate student at Berkeley, and still has Mom and Dad's credit card. In addition, Mary and Jim bought him a new car, and they pay for his gas. Because of his parents' enabling, Brendan is unable to manage his own financial responsibilities.

There is much middle ground between Hettleman's style and that of Mary and Jim, but Colorado State University retired administrator Jill Kreutzer agrees that parents need to teach their children budgeting from an early age. "Parents need to start early and help their children be financially responsible," she said. "That is tough, because parents are often not living financially responsible themselves."

While it may be tough to teach fiscal responsibility, there are many tools available online. Just search for "kids budgeting," "kids allowance," or something similar and thousands of Web sites are there for the viewing. Advice pours from these Web sites, including formulas for figuring out allowances for different ages, kid budget sheets, and college budget programs. No matter what age, get started teaching money management to your child. If she is in middle or high school, a great place to start is with a budget and a debit card. Discuss the terms, agree on a monthly amount you will deposit in the account, then let your child use the debit card. She will learn quickly how fast the money can disappear.

An alternative to the debit card is a checking account or a prepaid credit card. They work similarly to the debit card; it is up to you to decide which is the best tool. The most important thing: stick to the budget—don't give in.

Cathy and her husband had little trouble teaching their two sons to budget. Their daughter, however, was another story. After two years of Mariah's constant begging for clothing, accessories, makeup, and Archie comic books, Cathy put Mariah on a budget when she turned fourteen. Mariah was responsible for buying all her clothing except underwear, one pair of school shoes, and athletic team apparel. She was also responsible for her own entertainment expenses, cosmetics, snacks outside of home or school, and those Archie comic books. At first, Mariah was excited--$60 a month, with $5 toward savings, sounded like a lot. The first month, Mariah went to a concert and bought a $30 T-shirt. Within two weeks, she had spent all but $5 of her budget, but she still wanted to go shopping for back-to-school clothes. Cathy agreed to lend her the next month's budget toward school clothes. When Mariah started pleading for an $80 pair of jeans, Cathy held her ground. In tears, Mariah left the store and finally bought a $27 pair of jeans at JC Penny.

Another expense for which Mariah was responsible was her text messages on the cell phone she was given on her fourteenth birthday. Mariah agreed to pay $5 per month for two hundred text messages. In the third week, agitated and frustrated, Mariah announced that she couldn't possibly be expected to limit herself to two hundred text messages per month. She announced that she was willing to give up as much of her budget as necessary to gain unlimited text messaging. After giving Mariah a cooling-off period, Cathy asked her if she indeed was willing to give up $20 per month of her budget for one thing. Mariah agreed that was too much to lose, and compromised on a $10 plan that gave her more text messaging, but not unlimited. Cathy said she would wait to see how things turned out because she believed Mariah had a lot more to experience before she learned how to handle a budget. "Mariah doesn't like this budget idea anymore, and there are still battles to fight over spending," Cathy said. "But hopefully she will get it before she is ready for college."

Remember that all those challenges you face teaching your children to budget as middle-schoolers will pay off once they are ready to look at financing a college education. If your budget education worked, your students should be fairly reasonable when it comes to divvying up college expenses. He will know how to manage his money, she will appreciate the value of her education, and they will both have a much smoother financial transition to life beyond school.

Preparing Your Teenager: Money Management

College will not have gotten cheaper by the time you read this chapter, so start preparing now. Research savings, scholarships, loans, and other funding sources early in your student's high school years. Teach your student the importance of budgeting and saving, and the dangers of credit cards and loaning money. Give your teenager the responsibility of accounting for his spending, and let him try balancing a part-time job and schoolwork. With your guidance, your teenager will be ready for the financial responsibilities he will face in college and life beyond high school.

1) Teach your teenager the importance of budgeting and how to do it.

Challenge	Solution
Your teenager constantly asks you for money—for anything from movie tickets to a new hoodie she just can't live without. You have a weakly structured allowance program but nothing in place to teach her to budget.	Your teenager needs to be on a budget. First make a list of the things you are willing to pay for: certain clothing items, sports fees, etc. Calculate how much clothing you think she needs to buy over a given period of time, then research the costs of such items. Calculate the amount you are willing to give her for entertainment and other extras. Include savings in your planning as she will definitely need something to start with when she goes away to college. Also consider having her give a percentage to a charity or volunteer at a local organization in lieu of giving cash. Present her with the plan, discuss, make reasonable adjustments, and keep an account of all transactions. Then stick to the budget.
A budget was drawn and accepted by your teenager over a year ago, but she still comes asking for extra every month. She often wears you down.	Go back to the budget and re-evaluate. Ask her for an itemized spending of her money—there most likely are areas where she is spending without considering the consequences. Some readjustment of the budget may be necessary, but help her see where she is spending money without thinking about her budget first. Also consider suggesting she look for a part-time job. The job will give her more responsibility and she most likely will have a different attitude toward money she earns herself.

Challenge	Solution
As you are paying bills, your teenager comes asking for money. Exasperated, you shout something about how "money doesn't grow on trees."	Instead of getting upset with the poorly timed request, use this as a learning opportunity. Tell your teenager that he needs to understand how expensive everyday living is. Show him your mortgage bill, your utility bills, your garbage collection bills, etc. Have him multiply those numbers by 12 to understand the yearly cost. Then explain your credit card bill and show him the minimum payment, as well as the charges for late fees and interest rates. Again, have him do the math on interest rates to understand the concept. If you keep a budget yourself, pull it out and show him how hard it is to keep on track. Consider asking him to keep track of all the money he spends each month— he will be surprised!
Your teenager often asks for lunch money that he uses at fast food drive-throughs near school. He also likes to grab a pizza or burgers with friends most weekends. You feel your money is stretched thin by his requests.	Tell him no more money for food out until he completes some research. Have him write out how much his favorite foods cost, making sure he includes tax and any tips. Then send him to the grocery store to write down the prices of ingredients to make those same meals. (Avoid expensive prepared foods.) Together figure out how many meals he can make from the food purchased at the grocery store. Armed with this revealing information, tell him how much food allowance you will front. The rest is up to him.

2) Introduce your teenager to bank accounts and debit cards.

Challenge	Solution
For a couple of years, your teenager has done reasonably well with an allowance and a budget. In the summer, he lands a good job and now needs a bank account.	This is a great time for your teenager to learn about checking and savings accounts, and debit cards. Take him to the bank and have the bank representative explain to him how the accounts work. Make sure he understands why and how to record his deposits and debits. Make sure he understands that his debit card is not a credit card. Check in with him every week or so to see how things are going with his record keeping and savings.
One of your teenager's friends has her own credit card and your daughter thinks she should have one now that she has a part-time job. You struggle with credit card debt yourself and know your teenager is not ready for such a responsibility.	Be honest with your teenager about your own struggles. Show her your credit card statements and help her calculate how much interest you owe—then explain what you are doing to curb your credit card use. Explain to her how easy it is to overspend with a credit card and that the temptation would be hard for her to overcome. Insist she try a debit card instead and that she keep accurate records of her transactions. Go over those records with her periodically.

3) Teach your teenager about the dangers of lending and borrowing.

Challenge	Solution
Your teenager is a generous, friendly kid. He asks a few too many times for extra money because he loaned some of his allowance to a friend. When you ask when he will be repaid, your teenager replies: "Don't worry. He'll pay me back."	Admire your teenager's willingness to help a friend, but admit that you are alarmed at how easily he lends money. Tell him that he must keep a strict accounting of the money you've already handed out. Ask him if there are other ways to help a needy friend other than lending money. If he insists on continuing, tell him he must set up a repayment schedule with the friend—he can blame his parents for it. Tell him you won't be giving him anymore money until he collects repayment from his friends.
Although your teenager is on a budget, you are suspicious of how much he spends—it doesn't add up. You confront him and find out he has been borrowing money from friends, but has yet to pay much of it back.	Tell your son that his borrowing must stop. Explain the dangers and consequences of defaulting on a loan in the "real world." Review his budget and ask for an accounting of his spending. Insist he have receipts for all his purchases until he can show more responsibility in his spending. It may be necessary to check with him daily until he gets his spending under control. Help him work out a repayment schedule to his friends. Consider having him look for a part-time job or find jobs around the house for which you can pay him. Slowly give him more control over his funds as he learns responsible spending.

4) Help your teenager prepare for the financial responsibilities of college.

Challenge	Solution
Your teenager has her heart set on going to college, but money is tight. You finally tell her that you cannot fund much of her college education.	What you can do is start researching how it can be paid for. Have her talk with her school counselor about scholarships and grants. Recommend she open a profile with www.Fastweb.com or some other reputable scholarship search engine. There are many scholarships she can apply for earlier than her senior year. Start filling out the lengthy FAFSA application, and research loan options. If she knows what school she hopes to attend, research the financial aid provided by that institution. Start this research process early in your teenager's high school years.
Your teenager is on a budget, but she saves very little money. You know that she will need savings when she goes to college.	This is a good time to discuss what you will pay for and what she will pay for when she goes to college. Make a list of expenses that includes food, entertainment, transportation, clothing, and other costs besides tuition, books, and room and board. Be clear as to which expenses she will be responsible for. Ask her how she plans to prepare for those expenses. Discuss her efforts to save and help her move more cash in that direction. Ask her to consider a part-time or summer job and commit a percentage of her wages to savings.

Challenge	Solution
Although your teenager is a good student, you feel it is too much pressure for him to hold a job during the school year. He, however, wants a part-time job and argues that he is quite capable.	Despite your hesitation, let him pursue this path. You can set limits on his job, such as the number of hours and what times he can work. Make a contract that states if he falls behind on his schoolwork, he will either give up the job or work fewer hours. His schoolwork is his first and most important job, but this will give him the opportunity to pace himself and determine his limitations. Also, insist that he put a percentage of his wages toward his college savings.

The earlier you teach your child about budgeting, saving, credit, and loaning, the more prepared she will be to successfully handle her own finances. Good financial modeling at home teaches your child to be a responsible purchaser, a savvy saver, and a creative budgeter. Regardless of your financial situation, start researching now the ways you and your student can pay for college. And remember, however you end up paying for your student's education, it is usually a solid, fruitful investment.

Chapter 10

Final Thoughts

The stadium is packed with families all waiting for the same moment. But for now, it is your son's turn and you watch, clap, and hoot—swelling with pride and a few tears—as he shakes the principal's hand and walks off the stage with his high school diploma. Draped around his neck is a silver cord indicating that he graduated with honors, and under his name in the program is the name of the three scholarships he scored. You smile, remembering how hard you pushed him to research scholarships and loans.

In three weeks, you and he will travel to his college of choice, an in-state university, for orientation. His 3.8 grade point average; high SAT scores; and participation in student council, jazz band, wrestling, the Spanish club, Scouts, school-sponsored travel, and community service all helped clinch his admission to the three schools for which he applied. He has $2,000 saved from summer jobs, and he will add to that with the summer job ahead.

He has done well and you believe he is prepared for college, but that preparation wasn't without its tribulations. There were the two traffic tickets that raised his insurance rates and sent him into a frenzy when you reminded him of the driving contract that gave him the responsibility for the increase in his rates. There was the night last summer when he told you he was spending the night with his best friend, only to be caught by adults at a party with beer in hand and the distinct odor of marijuana in the air. There was the demanding chemistry teacher with whom he struggled, then begged you to ask the school administrators to switch him to another teacher's class. There were some missed curfews, all-nighters because he put off a project until the last minute, the constant badgering to get him to do his share of chores around the house, and the effort it took you to stay semiconsistent with consequences and expectations.

In other words, he's a pretty typical teenager. Congratulations! You've done well in preparing him to be ready, willing, and able to succeed in college.

Even if your teenager did not do as well as the one described above, if you have modeled problem solving, if you made expectations clear and have tried to be consistent—most of the time—with consequences, if you were involved in your teenager's education as well as social life, and if you gave your teenager graduated responsibilities, then congratulations to you also. Raising teenagers is a tough job, and preparing them for success in college and life beyond high school is never a straight and easy path to follow.

Although preparing for a successful college experience can certainly be overwhelming, remember that much of the skills your fledgling will need are basic—skills that you have been teaching since your teenager was a toddler. When those kids reach the teenage years, it begins to look as if that son was raised in another family or that daughter on another planet. Take heart that you aren't the only one feeling that way, and that most of those basics are still with them—just buried a bit.

Be aware of the skills your teenager will need to succeed in college, and start working now to review those skills or teach them for the first time. Once you are aware of the issues raised in this book, you have taken the first step to preparing your teenager to be ready, willing, and able to succeed in college and beyond.

Resources

The following resources were used in the research for this book.

Parenting

Marano, Hara Estroff. "A Nation of Wimps," Psychology Today, Nov. 1, 2004, http://www.psychologytoday.com/articles/200411/nation-wimps.

Stearns, Peter. Anxious Parenting: A History of Modern Childrearing in America. New York: New York University Press, 2003.

Wolf, Anthony E. Get Out of My Life, but First Could You Drive Me and Cheryl to the Mall? New York: Farrar, Straus and Giroux, 2002.

Gap Year

AmeriCorps, http://www.americorps.gov/

Dynamy, http://www.dynamy.org/

Reading

SQR3 (Survey, Question, Read, Recite, Review) method of reading, http://www.educatoral.com.SQUR3.html

Researching Colleges and Universities

College Board, http://www.collegeboard.com/.

Farr, J. Michael, and LaVerne L. Ludden. Best Jobs for the 21st Century. St. Paul, MN: Jist Publishing, 2006.

Fogg, Neeta P., Paul Harrington, and Thomas Harrington. College Majors Handbook with Real Career Paths and Payoffs: The Actual Jobs, Earnings, and Trends for Graduates of 60 College Majors. St. Paul, MN: Jist Publishing, 2004.

Fiske Guide to Colleges. Naperville, IL: Sourcebooks, 2011.

Fiske Guide to Getting into the Right College. Naperville, IL: Sourcebooks, 2010.

Kravets, Maybeth, and Imy Wax. K & W Guide to Colleges for Students with Learning Disabilities. Princeton, NJ: Princeton Review, 2010.

Peterson's Guides:

- 440 Great Colleges for Top Students
- Christian Colleges and Universities
- Colleges for Students with Learning Disabilities or AD/HD
- Green Jobs for a New Economy: The Career Guide to Energy Opportunities
- Guide to Four-Year Colleges
- Study Abroad
- Two-Year Colleges

Pope, Loren. Colleges That Change Lives: 40 Schools That Will Change the Way You Think About Colleges. New York: Penguin Books, 2006.

Princeton Review Guides:

- Complete Book of Colleges
- Guide to Studying Abroad
- Paying for College without Going Broke
- The Best 373 Colleges

University Visitors Network. A comprehensive college resource, http://www.universityvisitorsnetwork.com

Crime Statistics Resources

Bureau of Justice Statistics, http://www.bjs.ojp.usdoj.gov/

FBI Uniform Crime Report, http://www.fbi.gov/ucr/ucr.htm
Jeanne Clery Disclosure of Campus Security Policy and Campus Crime
Statistics Act (the Clery Act), http://www.securityoncampus.org/index.
php?option=com_content&view=article&id=271&Itemid=60.
National Institute of Alcohol Abuse and Alcoholism,
http://www.niaaa.nih.gov/
U.S. Department of Education, http://www.ope.ed.gov/security/

Privacy Laws

Family Educational Rights and Privacy Act (FERPA),
http://www2.ed.gov/policy/gen/guid/fpco/ferpa/index.html
The Health Insurance Portability and Accountability Act (HIPAA),
http://www.hhs.gov/ocr/privacy/

Alcohol and Drug Education Programs

Phoenix House: Facts on Tap and Transitions,
http://www.factsontap.org/

Financial Resources

529 accounts:
529 Accounts: Financial Aid For College, http://www.529accounts.com/
CollegeInvest, http://www.collegeinvest.org/
Savingforcollege.com, http://www.savingforcollege.com/intro_to_529s/
what-is-a-529-plan.php
U.S. Securities and Exchange Commission,
http://www.sec.gov/investor/pubs/intro529.htm
Budgeting:

FamilyEducation, http://life.familyeducation.com/money-and-kids/teen/34462.html

MoneyInstructor.com, http://www.moneyinstructor.com/budgeting.asp

Coverdell Education Savings Account:

Internal Revenue Service, http://www.irs.gov/newsroom/article/0,,id=107636,00.html

Savingforcollege.com,

http://www.savingforcollege.com/coverdell_esas/

Loans:

Free Application for Federal Student Aid (FAFSA):

http://www.fafsa.ed.gov/

Sallie Mae: https://www.salliemae.com/

Scholarship search:

Fastweb, http://www.fastweb.com/

Uniform Gift to Minors Account:

Bankrate.com,http://www.bankrate.com/brm/news/investing/20000517b.asp

FinAid, http://www.finaid.org/savings/ugma.phtml

Index